180 Days of Social-Emotional Learning for Third Grade

Kristin Kemp, M.A.Ed.

Consultants

Kris Hinrichsen, M.A.T., NBCT
Teacher and Educational Consultant
Anchorage School District

Amy Zoque
Teacher and Instructional Coach
Ontario Montclair School District

Publishing Credits

Corinne Burton, M.A.Ed., *Publisher*
Emily R. Smith, M.A.Ed., *VP of Content Development*
Lynette Ordoñez, *Content Specialist*
David Slayton, *Assistant Editor*
Jill Malcolm, *Multimedia Specialist*

Image Credits: all images from iStock and/or Shutterstock

Social-Emotional Learning Framework

The CASEL SEL framework and competencies were used in the development of this series.
© 2020 The Collaborative for Academic, Social, and Emotional Learning

Shell Education

A division of Teacher Created Materials
5482 Argosy Avenue
Huntington Beach, CA 92649-1039
www.tcmpub.com/shell-education
ISBN 978-1-0876-4972-6
© 2022 Shell Educational Publishing, Inc

Table of Contents

Introduction

"SEL is the process through which all young people and adults acquire and apply the knowledge, skills, and attitudes to develop healthy identities, manage emotions and achieve personal and collective goals, feel and show empathy for others, establish and maintain supportive relationships, and make responsible and caring decisions." (CASEL 2020)

Social-emotional learning (SEL) covers a wide range of skills that help people improve themselves and get fulfilment from their relationships. They are the skills that help propel us into the people we want to be. SEL skills give people the tools to think about the future and manage the day-to-day goal setting to get where we want to be.

The National Commission for Social, Emotional, and Academic Development (2018) noted that children need many skills, attitudes, and values to succeed in school, future careers, and life. "They require skills such as paying attention, setting goals, collaboration and planning for the future. They require attitudes such as internal motivation, perseverance, and a sense of purpose. They require values such as responsibility, honesty, and integrity. They require the abilities to think critically, consider different views, and problem solve." Explicit SEL instruction will help students develop and hone these important skills, attitudes, and values.

Daniel Goleman (2005), a social scientist who popularized SEL, adds, "Most of us have assumed that the kind of academic learning that goes on in school has little or nothing to do with one's emotions or social environment. Now, neuroscience is telling us exactly the opposite. The emotional centers of the brain are intricately interwoven with the neocortical areas involved in cognitive learning." As adults, we may find it difficult to focus on work after a bad day or a traumatic event. Similarly, student learning is impacted by their emotions. By teaching students how to deal with their emotions in a healthy way, they will reap the benefits academically as well.

SEL is doing the work to make sure students can be successful at home, with their friends, at school, in sports, in relationships, and in life. The skills are typically separated into five competencies: self-awareness, self-management, social awareness, relationship skills, and responsible decision-making.

Social-Emotional Competencies

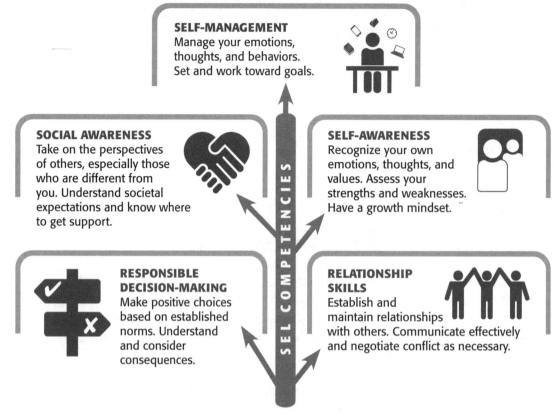

SELF-MANAGEMENT
Manage your emotions, thoughts, and behaviors. Set and work toward goals.

SOCIAL AWARENESS
Take on the perspectives of others, especially those who are different from you. Understand societal expectations and know where to get support.

SELF-AWARENESS
Recognize your own emotions, thoughts, and values. Assess your strengths and weaknesses. Have a growth mindset.

RESPONSIBLE DECISION-MAKING
Make positive choices based on established norms. Understand and consider consequences.

RELATIONSHIP SKILLS
Establish and maintain relationships with others. Communicate effectively and negotiate conflict as necessary.

SEL COMPETENCIES

Each SEL competency helps support child development in life-long learning. SEL helps students develop the skills to have rich connections with their emotional lives and build robust emotional vocabularies. These competencies lead to some impressive data to support students being successful in school and in life.

- Students who learn SEL skills score an average of 11 percentage points higher on standardized tests.

- They are less likely to get office referrals and will spend more time in class.

- These students are more likely to want to come to school and report being happier while at school.

- Educators who teach SEL skills report a 77 percent increase in job satisfaction. (Durlack, et al. 2011)

Your SEL Skills

Educators, parents, and caretakers have a huge part to play as students develop SEL skills. Parker Palmer (2007) reminds us that what children do is often a reflection of what they see and experience. When you stay calm, name your feelings, practice clear communication, and problem-solve in a way that students see, then they reflect that modeling in their own relationships. As you guide students in how to handle conflicts, you can keep a growth mindset and know that with practice, your students can master any skill.

Scenarios

There are many benefits to teaching SEL, from how students behave at home to how they will succeed in life. Let's think about how children with strong SEL skills would react to common life experiences.

At Home

Kyle wakes up. He uses self-talk and says to himself, *I am going to do my best today.* He gets out of bed, picks out his own clothes to wear, and gets ready. As he sits down for breakfast, his little sister knocks over his glass of milk. He thinks, *Uggh, she is so messy! But that's ok—it was just an accident.* Then, he tells his parent and helps clean up the mess.

When his parent picks Kyle up from school, Kyle asks how they are feeling and answers questions about how his day has gone. He says that he found the reading lesson hard, but he used deep breathing and asked questions to figure out new words today.

As his family is getting dinner ready, he sees that his parent is making something he really doesn't like. He stomps his foot in protest, and then he goes to sit in his room for a while. When he comes out, he asks if they can make something tomorrow that he likes.

When he is getting ready for bed, he is silly and playful. He wants to read and point out how each person in the book is feeling. His parent asks him how he would handle the problem the character is facing, and then they talk about the situation.

At School

Cynthia gets to school a little late, and she has to check into the office. Cynthia is embarrassed about being late but feels safe at school and knows that the people there will welcome her with kindness. She steps into her room, and her class pauses to welcome her. Her teacher says, "I'm so glad you are here today."

Cynthia settles into her morning work. After a few minutes, she comes to a problem she doesn't know how to solve. After she gives it her best try, she asks her teacher for some help. Her teacher supports her learning, and Cynthia feels proud of herself for trying.

As lunchtime nears, Cynthia realizes she forgot her lunch in the car. She asks her teacher to call her mom. Her mom says she can't get away and that Cynthia is going to have to eat the school lunch today. Cynthia is frustrated but decides that she is not going to let it ruin her day.

As she is getting ready for school to end, her teacher invites the class to reflect about their day. What is something they are proud of? What is something they wished they could do again? Cynthia thinks about her answers and shares with the class.

These are both pretty dreamy children. The reality is that the development of SEL skills happens in different ways. Some days, students will shock you by how they handle a problem. Other times, they will dig in and not use the skills you teach them. One of the benefits of teaching SEL is that when a student is melting down, your mindset shifts to *I wonder how I can help them learn how to deal with this* rather than *I'm going to punish them so they don't do this again.* Viewing discipline as an opportunity to teach rather than punish is critical for students to learn SEL.

How to Use This Book

Using the Practice Pages

This series is designed to support the instruction of SEL. It is not a curriculum. The activities will help students practice, learn, and grow their SEL skills. Each week is set up for students to practice all five SEL competencies.

 Day 1—Self-Awareness

 Day 2—Self-Management

 Day 3—Social Awareness

 Day 4—Relationship Skills

 Day 5—Responsible Decision-Making

Each of the five competencies has subcategories that are used to target specific skills each day. See the chart on pages 10–11 for a list of which skills are used throughout the book.

Each week also has a theme. These themes rotate and are repeated several times throughout the book. The following themes are included in this book:

- self
- friends
- family
- neighborhood
- community
- school

This book also features one week that focuses on online safety.

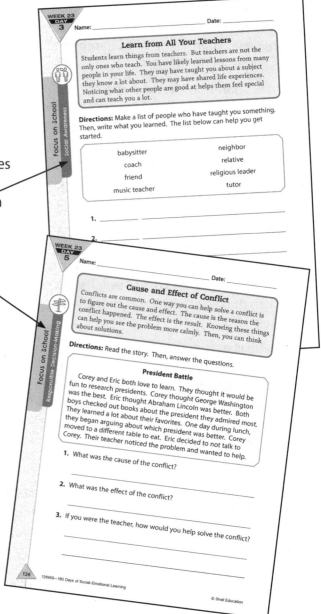

How to Use This Book *(cont.)*

Using the Resources

Rubrics for connecting to self, relating to others, and making decisions can be found on pages 198–200 and in the Digital Resources. Use the rubrics to consider student work. Be sure to share these rubrics with students so that they know what is expected of them.

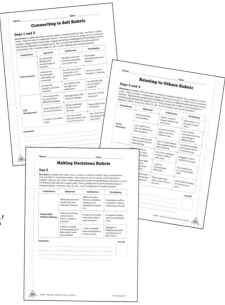

Diagnostic Assessment

Educators can use the pages in this book as diagnostic assessments. The data analysis tools included with this book enable teachers or parents/caregivers to quickly assess students' work and monitor their progress. Educators can quickly see which skills students may need to target further to develop proficiency.

Students will learn how to connect with their own emotions, how to connect with the emotions of others, and how to make good decisions. Assess student learning in each area using the rubrics on pages 198–200. Then, record their overall progress on the analysis sheets on pages 201–203. These charts are also provided in the Digital Resources as PDFs and Microsoft Excel® files.

To Complete the Analyses:

- Write or type students' names in the far-left column. Depending on the number of students, more than one copy of each form may be needed.

- The weeks in which students should be assessed are indicated in the first rows of the charts. Students should be assessed at the ends of those weeks.

- Review students' work for the day(s) indicated in the corresponding rubric. For example, if using the Making Decisions Analysis sheet for the first time, review students' work from Day 5 for all six weeks.

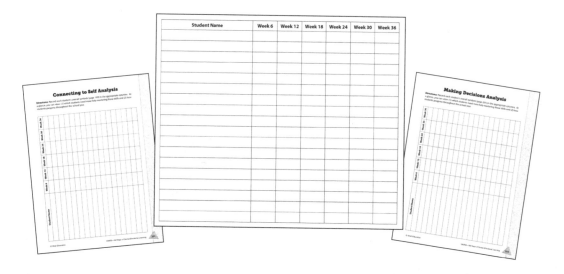

Integrating SEL into Your Teaching

Student self-assessment is key for SEL skills. If students can make accurate evaluations of how they are feeling, then they can work to manage their emotions. If they can manage their emotions, they are more likely to have better relationship skills and make responsible decisions. Children can self-assess from a very young age. The earlier you get them into this practice, the more they will use it and benefit from it for the rest of their lives. The following are some ways you can quickly and easily integrate student self-assessment into your daily routines.

Feelings Check-Ins

Using a scale can be helpful for a quick check-in. After an activity, ask students to rate how they are feeling. Focusing students' attention on how they are feeling helps support their self-awareness. Discuss how students' feelings change as they do different things. Provide students with a visual scale to support these check-ins. These could be taped to their desks or posted in your classroom. Full-color versions of the following scales can be found in the Digital Resources.

- **Emoji:** Having students point to different emoji faces is an easy way to use a rating scale with young students.

- **Symbols:** Symbols, such as weather icons, can also represent students' emotions.

- **Color Wheel:** A color wheel, where different colors represent different emotions, is another effective scale.

- **Numbers:** Have students show 1–5 fingers, with 5 being *I'm feeling great* to 1 being *I'm feeling awful.*

Reflection

Reflecting is the process of looking closely or deeply at something. When you prompt students with reflection questions, you are supporting this work. Here is a list of questions to get the reflection process started:

- What did you learn from this work?
- What are you proud of in this piece?
- What would you have done differently?
- What was the most challenging part?
- How could you improve this work?
- How did other people help you finish this work?
- How will doing your best on this assignment help you in the future?

Pan Balance

Have students hold out their arms on both sides of their bodies. Ask them a reflection question that has two possible answers. Students should respond by tipping one arm lower than the other (as if one side of the scale is heavier). Here are some example questions:

- Did you talk too much or too little?
- Were you distracted or engaged?
- Did you rush or take too much time?
- Did you stay calm or get angry?
- Was your response safe or unsafe?

Calibrating Student Assessments

Supporting student self-assessment means calibrating their thinking. You will have students who make mistakes but evaluate themselves as though they have never made a mistake in their lives. At the other end of the spectrum, you will likely see students who will be too hard on themselves. In both these cases, having a periodic calibration can help to support accuracy in their evaluations. The *Calibrating Student Assessments* chart is provided in the Digital Resources (calibrating.pdf).

Teaching Assessment

In addition to assessing students, consider the effectiveness of your own instruction. The *Teaching Rubric* can be found in the Digital Resources (teachingrubric.pdf). Use this tool to evaluate your SEL instruction. You may wish to complete this rubric at different points throughout the year to track your progress.

Skills Alignment

Each activity in this book is aligned to a CASEL competency. Within each competency, students will learn a variety of skills. Here are some of the important skills students will practice during the year.

Self-Awareness	
Identifying Emotions	Naming Emotions
Personal Traits	Intensity of Emotions
Self-Advocacy	Personal Values
Personal Identity	Curiosity
Growth Mindset	Traditions
Cultural Identity	Being Open-Minded
Connecting Feelings to Actions	Bravery

Self-Management	
Managing Emotions	Using Calendars
Integrity	I-Messages
Following Rules	Motivation
Honesty	Dealing with Stress
Setting Goals	Self-Talk
Courage	Organization
Calming Down	Trying New Things
Visualization	Self-Discipline

Social Awareness	
Helping Others	Empathy
Understanding Differences	Noticing Others' Needs
Reading Expressions	Compassion
Identifying Others' Emotions	Identifying Others' Strengths
Appropriate Behavior	Reading Body Language
Seeing Others' Perspectives	Learning from Others
Gratitude	Understanding Bias

Skills Alignment *(cont.)*

Relationship Skills	
Compliments	Causes and Effects
Solving Problems and Conflicts	Leadership
Understanding Cultures	Nonverbal Communication
Active Listening	Paraphrasing
Teamwork	Types of Solutions
Resisting Peer Pressure	Types of Communication
Advocating for Others	Effective Communication

Responsible Decision-Making	
Being Open-Minded	Evaluating the Size of Problems
Solving Problems	Weighing Different Options
Evaluating Ideas and Solutions	Mediating
Anticipating Consequences	Making Amends
Compromise	Evaluating Sources
Using Data	Causes and Effects of Conflicts
Reflecting	Making Good Choices

Name: Ah

Date: _____

Time for Your Emotions

You can have a lot of ups and downs in one day. It is normal to feel a lot of emotions in a single day.

Focus on Self

Self-Awareness

Directions: Write the letter that matches how you feel at each time of day.

A

C

B

D

1. waking up 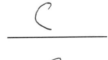 C

2. cleaning your room C

3. doing homework A

4. playing with friends D

5. getting ready for bed D

Name: _____ Date: _____

Calming Breaths

Breathing is a great way to manage your feelings. Deep belly breathing can help if you are angry, anxious, or scared. It can calm your mind and body.

Directions: Follow the directions to practice belly breathing. Then, answer the questions.

Belly Breathing

Step 1: Sit up straight with one hand on your chest and one hand on your belly.

Step 2: Breathe in deeply through your nose for four counts. Try to breathe using your belly. The hand on your chest should not move much, but the hand on your belly should move out. It might take a bit of practice!

Step 3: Breathe out through your mouth for four counts. The hand on your chest should not move much, but the hand on your belly should move in.

Step 4: Repeat until you feel more relaxed.

1. How did you feel after doing belly breathing?

good, and sad.

_____

2. When could belly breathing help manage your emotions?

calm.

_____

Name: _____ **Date:** _____

Show Others the Whole You

Words are one way to communicate with others. Your face and body also show how you feel.

Directions: Draw how you would feel in each situation.

1.

You must give a speech in front of the school.

3.

Your younger sister breaks your brand-new drone.

2.

You open a gift, and a puppy is inside the box.

4.

You win first place in the city spelling bee.

Name: _____ Date: _____

The Joy of Compliments

A compliment is something nice you say to someone. They are nice to hear. They can boost your self-esteem. Giving one can make you feel good, too. The best ones are honest and specific.

Focus on Self

Relationship Skills

Directions: Work with a partner to give each other compliments. Then, answer the questions.

1. What compliment did you give?

_____

_____

_____

2. How did it feel?

_____

_____

3. What compliment did you receive?

_____

_____

4. How did it feel?

_____

_____

Name: _____ Date: _____

Try to Stay Open-Minded

Being open-minded means you will try new things. It can be scary to try things for the first time. But you will never know if you can do them until you try.

Directions: List three things you would like to try. They might be a sport or hobby, a type of food, or something else. Then, draw a picture of you trying one of your ideas.

1. _____

2. _____

3. _____

Name: _____ Date: _____

Your Traits and You

Everyone has traits. A trait is something that makes you unique. You are really good at some things. You likely struggle with other things. The people in your family might have traits different from yours. You can use your strengths to help one another.

Directions: Answer the questions about your traits.

1. What is one thing you do well?

_____

2. Draw yourself using that trait to help a family member.

3. What trait would you like to work on?

_____

4. Draw yourself working on that trait.

Focus on Family

Self-Awareness

Name: _____ Date: _____

Focus on Family

Self-Management

Show Integrity

Integrity means to be honest and fair. It is an important character trait. It isn't always easy. But it is the right thing to do.

Directions: Answer the questions about each event.

Cookies for Snack

Your aunt made a big batch of sugar cookies, your favorite. She said you could have two cookies. They were delicious, so you ate three. Later, your aunt asked how many cookies you ate.

1. What should you say to your aunt? Show integrity.

_____

_____

The Broken Vase

You knew you weren't supposed to kick the soccer ball in the house, but it was so much fun you couldn't help it. *Crash!* The ball flew through the air and smashed a vase on the table. You quickly swept up the broken pieces and put them in the trash. A few minutes later, your parent comes home from work.

2. What should you say to your parent? Show integrity.

_____

_____

126959—180 Days of Social-Emotional Learning

Name: _____ **Date:** _____

You Can Do One Thing

No one can do everything. But everyone can do one thing. Maybe more! Your family can work together. You can each do small things to make your home better.

Directions: Answer the questions to show how you can help your family. Then, draw a picture to show one of your ideas.

1. How can you show a family member kindness?

   _____

   _____

2. How can you help keep your home clean?

   _____

   _____

3. Draw yourself helping your family.

Name: _____ Date: _____

Time for Family Relationships

It is good to have strong relationships. All relationships are important. But the ones with your family are very important. You likely spend a lot of time with your family.

Directions: Complete the web with your name in the middle and the names of family members on the outside ovals. You may need to add ovals or leave some blank. Then, answer the question.

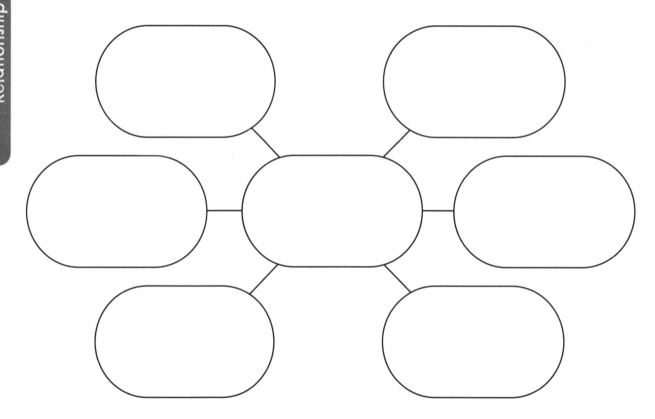

1. Choose one person from your web. How could you make your relationship with them better?

_____

_____

_____

Name: _____ **Date:** _____

Your Personal Solutions

Problems are a part of life. Some problems are personal, which means they only affect you. But they still need solutions.

Directions: Read the story. Then, answer the questions.

Sleepyhead

Josh rolled over in bed. He heard his mom calling his name from the bottom of the stairs. Sleepily, he opened one eye and glanced at the clock next to his bed. Then, he sat straight up in bed and threw back the covers. Josh would have to hurry or he was going to be late for school—again!

1. What is the problem in this story?

_____

_____

2. How could Josh solve the problem on his own?

_____

_____

3. How could Josh get help from his family to solve the problem?

_____

_____

Focus on Family

Responsible Decision-Making

Name: _____ Date: _____

A Recipe for Friendship

If friendship were a recipe, what would the ingredients be? Things in common? Being silly? Trust is important, too. If you trust your friends, you can feel more comfortable, valued, and supported.

Directions: Answer the questions about your friends.

1. Which friend can you trust most? Why do you trust that person?

_____

_____

2. Can your friends trust you? How do you know?

_____

_____

3. Draw yourself with a friend you trust.

Focus on Friends

Self-Awareness

Name: _____ **Date:** _____

Stay Safe Together

Being with friends is a lot of fun. You might go to someone's house, a park, or the playground at school and play together. It's important not only to have fun, but also to stay safe. Rules help keep people safe. Following the rules is a good way to manage your feelings and actions.

Directions: Write five safety rules for a place where you and a friend like to go together.

Safety Rules

1. _____

_____

2. _____

_____

3. _____

_____

4. _____

_____

5. _____

_____

Focus on Friends

Self-Management

Name: _____ Date: _____

Understanding Differences

Friends often have things in common. Maybe you both like the same sports or video games. But everyone is different. You and your friends will never be exactly alike. Understanding differences between people is good. It helps you to be a better friend.

Directions: Write a friend's name on the blank line. In the two outer circles, list your differences. In the middle circle, list things you have in common.

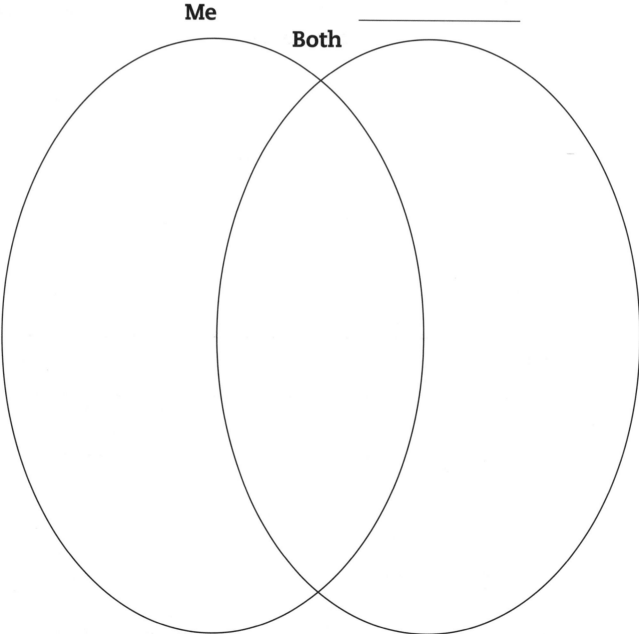

Me   Both   _____

126959—180 Days of Social-Emotional Learning   © Shell Education

Name: _____ Date: _____

The Best Conflicts

Even best friends don't always get along. Conflicts are normal. It is important to know how to solve them. If you are arguing with a friend, stay calm. Both of you should share how you feel. Then, try to find a solution. Remember, there isn't one right way to solve a conflict.

Directions: Write an ending to the story that shows how the friends find a solution.

The New Pencil Sharpener

Rahul was excited to show his new pencil sharpener to his best friend, Ruby. It was made for special charcoal pencils. Ruby loves to draw, so he knew she would like it. Rahul showed the pencil sharpener to Ruby and let her hold it. She picked up a regular pencil from her desk and began twisting it in the sharpener.

"Ruby, no!" Rahul gasped. "Regular pencils will bend the blade!"

They looked and saw that the blade was bent.

"It's ruined, Ruby," Rahul said angrily. "You broke it!"

Ruby scowled and said, "You never said a regular pencil would break it!"

_____

_____

_____

_____

Focus on Friends

Relationship Skills

Name: _____ Date: _____

Good and Bad Solutions

You make many decisions every day. You decide what to wear. You decide what to eat. You decide how to spend your free time. Sometimes, you might have to decide if an idea is good or bad. Good ideas might help people or make things better. Bad ideas might be dangerous or hurt people.

Directions: Circle whether each situation is a good idea or bad idea. Then, explain why.

1. Your friend hands you a birthday invitation. Only three people are invited. She asks you to put it in your backpack.

    good idea   bad idea

    _____

    _____

2. A man at the park asks your friend to help find his dog. Your friend wants you to help, too.

    good idea   bad idea

    _____

    _____

3. A classmate has not had a lunch to eat for a few days. Your friend says you should take the classmate to talk to the teacher.

    good idea   bad idea

    _____

    _____

Name: _____ **Date:** _____

Do Your Part

A community is made of many people. Each person needs to help make the community a good place to live. You are part of your community. So, you should do your part.

Directions: Draw something you could do for your community. Then, explain your drawing.

_____

_____

_____

_____

Name: _____ Date: _____

Honest Leaders

You should always try to be honest. Community leaders need to be really honest. A lot of people count on them.

Directions: Read the story. Then, answer the questions.

The Festival Promise

Mayor Patricia Hart had promised to hold a big fall festival. Then, she learned about an old bridge that needs repairs. Now, she has to use the festival money to fix the bridge. She is getting ready to give an interview on TV. Mayor Hart knows she will be asked about the festival. She is afraid to tell the truth.

1. Why is Mayor Hart afraid to tell the truth?

   _____

2. Why is it important for her to tell the truth?

   _____

3. How might people respond to her announcement?

   _____

   _____

4. Describe a time when you had to tell the truth even though it was hard.

   _____

   _____

Name: _____ Date: _____

Read Expressions

There are many different people in your community. It can be hard to know what they are thinking. But you can understand their expressions. That can help you know how they are feeling without saying a word.

Directions: Draw the expression on each face.

shy

friendly

lost

angry

Name: _____ Date: _____

Relationship Variety

There are a lot of people in your community. None of them are exactly the same. You likely know some of them better than others. It can be helpful to know a wide variety of people.

Directions: Write the names of three people you know in your community. Then, write two good things about each person.

1. Name: _____

- _____

- _____

2. Name: _____

- _____

- _____

3. Name: _____

- _____

- _____

Focus on Community

Relationship Skills

Name: _____ Date: _____

Big and Small Problems

Some problems are small. You can solve them on your own. Other problems are big. You might need help from a group of people or even a whole community to solve them.

Directions: Read the story, and underline the problem. Write two different solutions. Then, draw one of the solutions.

Help the Library!

Elias loves to read, but he's a little disappointed with his town's library. It seems like it never has the books he wants to read. Elias talks to a few friends at school. He even asks his older sister and her friends. They all agree the library does not have enough books. He talks to his mom about it. She says it is too big of a problem for them to solve on their own. If they want to make a change, they will need to work with the community.

Solution 1	Solution 2

Name: _____ Date: _____

Be an Advocate

An advocate is a person who works to support a person or group. They can also support a cause. You can be your own advocate. You can speak up and say what you need.

Directions: Read the scenarios. Write how each person could advocate for themselves.

1. Marcus works hard in math. But fractions are really hard. His teacher assigns homework and moves on to another topic. Marcus does not understand what he is supposed to do.

_____

_____

2. Bethany is playing outside with friends. They decide to ride their bikes, but she does not have a bike.

_____

_____

Directions: Describe a time when you advocated for yourself.

_____

_____

_____

Name: _____ **Date:** _____

Look to Set Goals

People can be successful in a lot of ways. Making goals and working hard will help you be successful. Before you set goals, look for the places in your life where you need them most.

Directions: Complete the web by listing parts of your life. Include things such as school and your hobbies or activities.

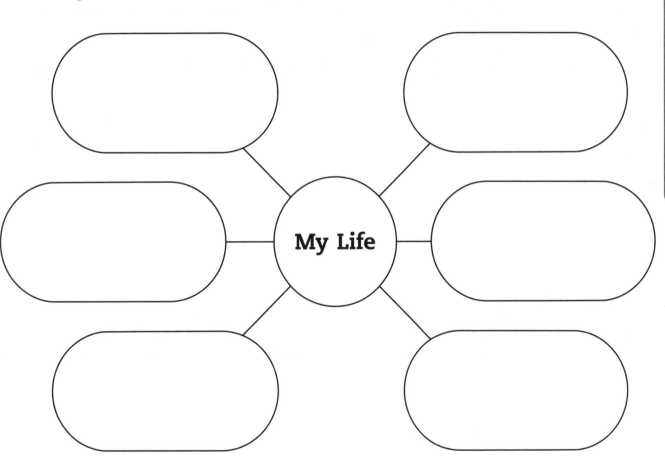

My Life

Directions: Draw a star next to one area from your web. Write a goal you can work on in that area.

_____

_____

Focus on Self

Self-Management

Name: _____ Date: _____

Look for Ways to Be Helpful

If you look, you will find chances to be helpful every day. A helpful person tries their best when they see chances to help. You can help others in big and small ways, too.

Directions: Draw a time you helped someone in the first box. Draw a way you could help someone tomorrow in the second box.

Name: _____ **Date:** _____

Your Cultural Competence

You have cultural competence if you know about a culture. Holidays are one part of culture. Some are religious. Some honor a person. Some honor an event. They are all part of a culture.

Directions: Answer the questions about a holiday or special event in your culture. Then, draw how you spend that day.

1. What holiday do you enjoy?

_____

2. Describe the holiday.

_____

_____

3. Why is this holiday important?

_____

_____

4. Draw how you spend the holiday.

Name: _____ Date: _____

Focus on Self

Responsible Decision-Making

Anticipate Consequences

Every decision has a consequence. Some of them are good, and some of them are not. Thinking about what might happen will help you make good decisions.

Directions: Write a possible consequence for each situation.

1. You stayed up late to finish reading a book.

   _____

   _____

2. You studied hard for your social studies quiz.

   _____

   _____

3. You ate your sister's candy bar.

   _____

   _____

4. You invited a new student to eat lunch with you.

   _____

   _____

   _____

© Shell Education

Name: _____ **Date:** _____

Your Neighborhood and You

Your family and your culture help make you who you are. Your neighborhood affects you, too. Many things about the way you are being raised will shape your beliefs. They can change the way you see the world.

Directions: Draw your neighborhood. Then, answer the questions.

```
┌ ─ ─ ─ ─ ─ ─ ─ ─ ─ ─ ─ ─ ─ ─ ─ ─ ─ ┐



│                                   │



└ ─ ─ ─ ─ ─ ─ ─ ─ ─ ─ ─ ─ ─ ─ ─ ─ ─ ┘
```

1. What is special about where you live?

_____

_____

2. What is one thing you wish was different about your neighborhood?

_____

_____

Name: _____ Date: _____

Courage

Trying something new can be scary. People often worry that something will be too hard or that they will fail. This keeps them from trying new things. But new things can be fun and exciting.

Directions: Read the story. Then, answer the questions.

The Dark Street

Kajal had just moved to her new home and was getting to know the neighborhood. So far, she liked it. But at night, everyone went inside and turned off their porch lights. Kajal remembered the way people would sit outside in the evenings on her old street. She and her friends would play together. Someone always turned on music. She missed that, and she wondered if her new neighbors would enjoy something similar. Kajal would like to make a change, but she was scared. After all, she was new and just a child.

1. How does Kajal feel about trying to make a change?

_____

2. What advice would you give to Kajal?

_____

_____

3. How could Kajal begin to make a change?

_____

_____

Look for Feelings on Faces

Sometimes, people say how they are feeling. Other times, you can tell by the look on their faces. The way a person acts can also let you know how they feel. If you pay attention when you walk down the street, you can learn a lot about your neighbors.

Focus on Neighborhood

Social Awareness

Directions: Write how you think each person is feeling.

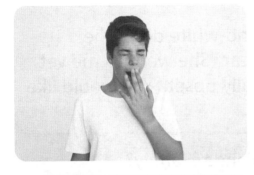

1. _____

   _____

   _____

2. _____

   _____

   _____

3. _____

   _____

   _____

4. _____

   _____

   _____

Name: _____ Date: _____

Help Your Neighbors

Neighbors need help with all sorts of things. There are many ways to show your neighbors you care. You can work to help the people around you.

Directions: Read the story. Then, answer the questions.

Hurt Panda

Panda is your neighbor's little black-and-white dog. She escaped from her yard and was hit by a car. She went to the vet and will be fine. But her family is still really upset. You would like to help Panda's family.

1. What are two ways you could help Panda's family?

   _____

   _____

2. Which idea do you like best? Why?

   _____

   _____

3. Draw yourself helping Panda and her family.

Name: _____ Date: _____

Compromise

People do not always agree. That can lead to arguments. A compromise is when each person gives something up in order to end the conflict. It is one way to solve a problem.

Directions: Read the story. Then, answer the questions.

Drum Dilemma

Alice lives in the apartment above Jamal. Alice is in a band and plays the drums. Jamal is a nurse and works nights at the hospital. Alice likes to practice drums after breakfast each day, but that is when Jamal gets home from work and is ready to sleep. Alice feels like she should be able to practice the drums when she wants. Jamal feels like he should be able to sleep when he wants. They cannot seem to agree.

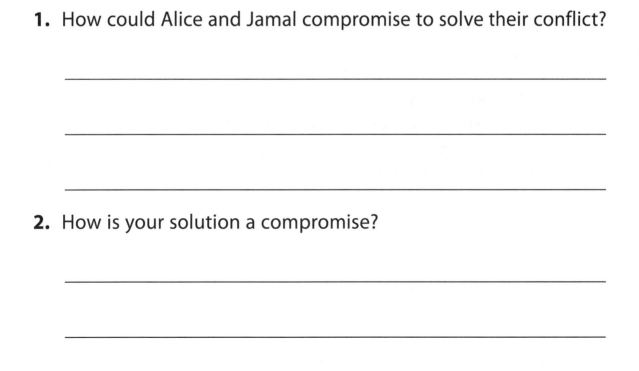

1. How could Alice and Jamal compromise to solve their conflict?

_____

_____

_____

2. How is your solution a compromise?

_____

_____

_____

Focus on Neighborhood

Responsible Decision-Making

Name: _____ Date: _____

Growth Mindset

Everyone has a mindset. Your mindset is all your beliefs and attitudes. A fixed mindset means you do not believe you can achieve more. A growth mindset means you think you can achieve more.

Directions: Read each story. Write whether the person has a fixed mindset or a growth mindset and how you know.

1. Liam struggles with math. He always does his homework, but he knows he'll never understand math.

_____

_____

_____

2. Sofia has a hard time writing. She has clever ideas, but she struggles with spelling and punctuation. Sofia knows she will get better at writing if she keeps trying.

_____

_____

_____

Name: _____ Date: _____

Collective Goals

People set goals when they want to accomplish things. A group of people can make a collective goal. This is when people work together to achieve something. Making a group goal can be challenging. It can be hard to work with a lot of people. Knowing how to create a group goal is a good skill.

Directions: Follow the steps to create a goal for your school.

Step 1: Think

Think about your school. Are there any problems? Brainstorm three things you would like to change.

_____

_____

_____

Step 2: Discuss

Share your ideas with a partner. Listen as they share their ideas. Choose one idea to share with the larger group.

Step 3: Choose

As a class, choose a good goal for your school. You may be able to pick one based on discussion. You might need to vote to choose one goal.

Step 4: Create

Write your class's goal for the school.

_____

_____

_____

Self-Management

Focus on School

Name: _____ Date: _____

Focus on School

Social Awareness

Rules of the Roads

Different places have their own rules. A library might have a rule to use a quiet voice. But that would not be a good rule at the park. Understanding different rules helps you know how you should behave in different places.

Directions: Circle whether each rule is for home, school, or both. Then, answer the question.

1. Raise your hand before you speak.   home   school   both

2. Clean up your mess.   home   school   both

3. Use kind words.   home   school   both

4. Put away your laundry.   home   school   both

5. Ask permission to use the restroom.   home   school   both

6. Why do schools and homes need different rules?

_____

_____

_____

Name: _____ Date: _____

Be an Active Listener

Hearing is not the same as listening. You might hear someone talking. But if you don't remember what they said, you may not have been listening. Active listening is a skill. It will help you communicate well.

Directions: Read about how to be an active listener. Then, write and draw tips about how to listen well.

Active Listening

You can learn to be an active listener. First, do not speak while the other person is talking. Concentrate on what they are saying. Second, use body language or facial expressions. This will help show you are listening. You might nod your head or lean closer. Finally, when they are finished talking, restate what they said. This will make sure you understand.

Focus on School

Relationship Skills

Name: _____ Date: _____

Focus on School

Responsible Decision-Making

Slow and Steady Decisions

Quick decisions are not always the best decisions. It is better to take the time to make a good choice. Look at data. Consider different options. Use information to make a good decision.

Directions: Imagine that you must choose a habitat to research. Complete the table to help you make a decision. Then, answer the question.

Question	Desert	Rain Forest
What would you like about researching this habitat?		
What about this habitat is most interesting to you?		
What are some disadvantages about researching this habitat?		

1. Which habitat would you choose to research? Why?

_____

_____

© Shell Education

Name: _____ **Date:** _____

Find Your Purpose

It takes a lot of people to make a community a good place to live. Children can help, too! You can use your talents in all sorts of ways.

Directions: Draw yourself helping your community. Then, write at least two sentences to explain your picture.

_____

_____

_____

_____

_____

Focus on Community

Self-Awareness

Name: _____ Date: _____

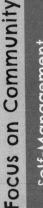

Manage Your Big Feelings

When you have big feelings, it's easy to have big reactions. Sadness, anger, and fear can be hard to manage. It's good to have strategies to calm your mind.

Directions: Read the story. Then, answer the questions.

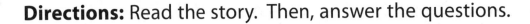

Andre's Anger

Andre and Micah were playing basketball at the park when Micah's older brother walked over with a few of his friends.

"Your turn is up," his brother called out. "It's our turn now."

"No way!" Micah yelled. "We've only been playing for 10 minutes!"

"Get off the court," his brother said.

"You're being a bully, and I'm going to tell Mom!" Micah said, waving his arm in the air.

Andre felt really angry because Micah's brother was always bossing them around. But, he closed his eyes, took a deep breath, and counted to five in his head.

"We aren't done playing," Andre said. His voice was calm, but firm. "You can play next."

1. How did Micah show his anger?

_____

2. How did Andre manage his anger?

_____

Name: _____ Date: _____

The Perspective of Others

Not everyone has the same ideas and opinions. You may not agree with someone. But you can try to see things from their perspective. That means you think about a topic the way the other person would. You still may not agree. But you might see why they have that belief.

Directions: Read the text. Then, answer the questions.

Two Choices

Someone gave a large amount of money to your community! The people can choose how to spend the money. But it has to be on something that many people can use. After a lot of debate, there are two choices. They will either build a skate park or a garden.

1. Would you choose a skate park or a garden? Why?

   _____

   _____

2. Why might someone choose the other option? Give two reasons.

   _____

   _____

3. Why is it good to be able to see things from another perspective?

   _____

   _____

Focus on Community

Social Awareness

Name: _____ Date: _____

Plan to Work as a Team

Working as a team is a great way to get a job done quickly. Teams work best if they have a plan and work effectively.

Directions: Write how each team could work together.

1.

_____

_____

_____

2.

_____

_____

_____

3.

_____

_____

_____

Name: _____ **Date:** _____

Think about the Consequences

You know that your actions have consequences. But some of your actions can affect more than just you. Some actions can affect your whole community. Thinking ahead can help you make better choices.

Directions: Read the story. Then, draw how Audrey's decision could affect others.

The City Pool

Audrey loves to swim at the city pool. One day, she arrived before lunch and saw some children already there. Audrey's favorite thing to do in the water is to float on her raft. Rafts are not allowed in the pool because they are too big. But the lifeguard doesn't come on duty for a few hours. She knows she could float for a little while before he comes to work.

Name: _____ Date: _____

Focus on Self
Self-Awareness

Your Interests and Your Purpose

There are so many ways for you to spend your days. Learning your interests will bring you purpose. Learning what makes you happy will bring you joy.

Directions: Draw yourself doing two things that make you feel good. Give each drawing a title.

_____

_____

Name: _____ Date: _____

Visualization

People can feel stress when they are angry or afraid. One way to manage that stress is to use visualization. This means you create a picture in your head of how the problem could be solved. It can help you feel a lot better.

Directions: After you read each situation, close your eyes. Visualize how you might solve the problem and feel better. Then, describe what you visualized.

1. Your sister let you borrow her headphones. You accidentally broke them. You are scared to tell her because you know she will be mad at you.

   _____

   _____

   _____

   _____

2. You and your best friend often hang out after school. The last few weeks, she has been playing with someone else. You feel sad because you are left out of the fun.

   _____

   _____

   _____

   _____

Name: _____ Date: _____

Focus on Self

Social Awareness

Look for Ways to Help

Everyone needs help sometimes. But a lot of people don't ask for it. If you look, you can find someone to help every day. Noticing people's needs and offering to help is very kind.

Directions: Write how you can help each person. Then, circle an idea you can do today.

Family Member	Friend
_____	_____
_____	_____
_____	_____
_____	_____
Neighbor	**Teacher**
_____	_____
_____	_____
_____	_____
_____	_____

Name: _____ **Date:** _____

Resist Peer Pressure

Peer pressure is when a group tries to get you to change your mind. Some peer pressure is good and helps you make good choices. But sometimes, peer pressure isn't so good. It can influence you to do something you know you should not do.

Directions: Read the story. Then, answer the questions.

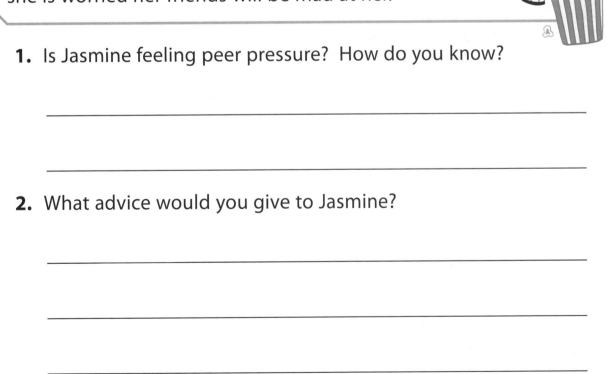

The Class Reward

Jasmine's class has earned a reward for good behavior. After lunch, the class will vote for either movie day or pajama day. Jasmine loves pajama day. But her two best friends want her to vote for movie day. Jasmine's friends have been talking to her all morning. They think movie day will be more fun and that Jasmine's vote will help their choice win. Jasmine isn't sure what to do. She would rather wear her pajamas, but she is worried her friends will be mad at her.

1. Is Jasmine feeling peer pressure? How do you know?

_____

_____

2. What advice would you give to Jasmine?

_____

_____

_____

_____

Name: _____ Date: _____

Reflect on Your Well-Being

Sometimes, it is helpful to reflect on your life. This means you think about what is going on in your life and how you feel about it. A reflection can help you understand yourself better.

Directions: Answer the questions. Then, use those ideas to write a reflection about how you are feeling at home or at school.

Focus on Self

Responsible Decision-Making

1. What makes you feel proud of yourself?

   _____

2. What makes you happy?

   _____

3. What makes you feel sad or anxious?

   _____

4. What would you like to do better?

   _____

My Reflection

_____

_____

_____

_____

Name: _____ **Date:** _____

> ## The Importance of Holidays
>
> Most families celebrate holidays. They are a part of their cultures. You can learn more about your holidays. This will help you learn about your culture.

Directions: Read the story. Then, answer the questions.

> ### Diwali
>
> Krish woke up early today. It's the first day of Diwali! His parents moved from India many years ago. But they still celebrate this holiday known as the Festival of Lights. Diwali lasts five days, and each day is special. Krish can't wait for the feast and fireworks on the third day. His aunts, uncles, and cousins all come to his house. Then, the next day, they celebrate the new year and give gifts to each other. The next five days will be awesome!

1. How does Krish feel about Diwali? How do you know?

_____

_____

2. Draw a holiday you celebrate.

Name: _____ Date: _____

Benefits of a Calendar

Families often have a lot of places to be. They need to stay organized. Using a calendar can help. Putting it where everyone can see it helps, too. Calendars make sure everyone gets to the right place at the right time.

Focus on Family

Self-Management

Directions: Study the family calendar. Then, answer the questions.

Monday	Tuesday	Wednesday	Thursday	Friday
9:30 a.m. Mom: book club 6:00 p.m. Luis: piano lesson	3:30 p.m. Maria: tutoring	1:15 p.m. Luis: dentist 5:30 p.m. Maria: soccer practice	12:00 p.m. Mom: volunteer 7:00 p.m. Luis: swim lesson	6:00 p.m. Family: dinner at Grandma's

1. What happens on Friday? Who is going?

   _____

2. When does Maria have tutoring?

   _____

3. What activities do you have during the week? How do you keep organized?

   _____

   _____

4. Where could you put a family calendar in your home?

   _____

Name: _____ Date: _____

Show Gratitude

When someone says or does something kind for you, it is nice to show gratitude. Gratitude means to be thankful. There are many ways to show gratitude. You could say thank you. You could mail a card. You could do something kind in return.

Directions: Read the text. Then, draw two ways the family could show gratitude.

An Act of Kindness

Tia's mom just had a baby. Things are very busy at her house now! Mrs. Point, their next-door neighbor, brought dinner to Tia and her family. They were so grateful for Mrs. Point's kindness. They want to show gratitude.

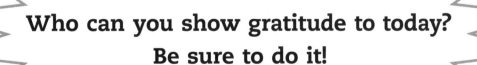

Who can you show gratitude to today? Be sure to do it!

Focus on Family
Social Awareness

Name: _____ Date: _____

Resolve Conflicts

Conflicts happen all the time. They even happen in families. It's okay for family members to have conflicts. They just need to know how to resolve them.

Focus on Family

Relationship Skills

Directions: Read the steps to resolve conflicts. Color each big letter. Then, use the letters to help you remember the steps.

 Ask what the problem is.

 Brainstorm ideas to solve the problem.

 Choose the best solution.

 Do it!

Directions: Draw a time you resolved a conflict with a family member.

Name: _____ Date: _____

Different-Sized Problems

Problems come in different sizes. Some problems might be big, and you will need an adult's help to solve them. Other problems are small and can be solved on your own. It is important to know the difference.

Directions: Circle whether each problem is big or small.

1. Your brother borrowed your markers without asking.   big   small

2. You didn't get to wear your favorite shirt.   big   small

3. Your dresser drawers are messy.   big   small

4. You fell off the swing and hurt your arm.   big   small

5. Your sister won't stop calling you mean names.   big   small

6. The battery on your device is getting low.   big   small

© Shell Education

Focus on Family

Responsible Decision-Making

Name: _____ Date: _____

Focus on Friends

Self-Awareness

Act on Your Emotions

The way we act can be connected to how we feel. A happy person and an angry person will act in different ways. If you see this link in your friends, you will be a better friend. You will be more aware of their emotions. You will be more aware of your emotions, too.

Directions: Match the behaviors to the emotions they show.

1. _____ kicking a chair, yelling

A. happy

2. _____ sitting alone, not talking to friends

B. sad

3. _____ groaning, rolling eyes

C. angry

4. _____ laughing, playing with friends

D. interested

5. _____ listening carefully, paying attention

E. frustrated

Name: _____ Date: _____

I-Messages

I-messages are a good way to manage your emotions. An I-message tells someone how you feel. Say *I* and then say your feelings. This works better than saying *you* if you are in an argument. I-messages tell how you feel. They can help keep you and others calm.

Directions: Rewrite each sentence to be an I-message. Follow the example.

Example

You always leave your toys in my room.

<u>I feel frustrated when you</u>

<u>leave your toys in my room.</u>

1. You always make fun of me when I trip and fall.

   _____

   _____

2. You don't take turns when we play video games.

   _____

   _____

Focus on Friends

Self-Management

Name: _____ Date: _____

Feel Empathy

Having empathy means you can tell how someone else feels. You do not need to have felt the same thing. But you can imagine how it would feel. Showing empathy can make you a better friend.

Directions: Write how you think each person feels.

1. Elliot's family adopted a puppy last night. He has been asking for a dog for over a year.

   _____

2. Malik studied for his spelling test. He got all the words right.

   _____

3. Alejandro has been saving for a new game. He went to the store to buy it, and it was sold out.

   _____

4. Heidi's mom is supposed to pick her up after school. Her mom is late and is not answering her phone.

   _____

5. Megan's friends are giggling and pointing in her direction.

   _____

   _____

Name: _____ Date: _____

Stand Up for Others

All people have rights. Rights are freedoms people should have. But sometimes, people are not given their rights. When that happens, they need someone to stand up for them.

Directions: Read the story. Then, answer the questions.

Riding Lessons

Margo and Tasha have been best friends for a long time and have a lot in common. They both love taking horseback riding lessons. Margo can't move her legs, so she uses a wheelchair. The barn where they take riding lessons has a new teacher. She says Margo can't ride anymore. She doesn't think Margo will be safe because of her disability. Tasha knows this is not fair!

1. Why does Tasha think it is not fair?

_____

_____

2. How could Tasha stand up for Margo's rights?

_____

_____

3. Describe a time when you stood up for another person.

_____

_____

Name: _____ Date: _____

The Causes and Effects of Problems

Think of a problem you have had. What caused the problem? This problem then likely had an effect on something else. Thinking about the causes and effects of problems can help you solve them.

Directions: Read the story. Write the cause and effect of the problem. Then, draw how you would solve it.

The Recess Problem

James told Lucas they could play soccer together at recess. Lucas was looking forward to recess all morning. At recess, James ran over to the kickball field and volunteered to be the pitcher. Lucas was mad, so he went over to talk to James. James said he had changed his mind. Lucas thought that was unfair, and the two friends argued.

Cause

_____

_____

_____

Effect

_____

_____

_____

Solution

126959—180 Days of Social-Emotional Learning   © Shell Education

Name: _____ Date: _____

Your Community Needs You

Communities need many people to keep them running smoothly. You have ideas and skills that can help.

Directions: Think about your community. List ideas for each topic. Then, answer the questions.

Problems	Ways to Volunteer
• _____	• _____
• _____	• _____
• _____	• _____

1. Circle one of your ideas from the table. How could you help with this topic?

   _____

   _____

2. Explain what you would do.

   _____

   _____

3. How would your idea help your community?

   _____

   _____

Focus on Community

Self-Awareness

Name: _____ **Date:** _____

Find Your Self-Motivation

Sometimes, you may not want to do your homework. You may not want to clean your room. Self-motivation is what pushes you to keep going.

Directions: Write what you would say to yourself in each situation to keep yourself motivated.

1. Your community is having a baking contest. You are excited to enter, but every time you try your recipe, something goes wrong. You feel frustrated and want to withdraw from the contest.

   _____

   _____

2. You are cleaning up litter in the park. It is a hot day, and you have been working all afternoon. You're hot, tired, and ready to quit. But the park is not clean yet.

   _____

   _____

3. Your community is holding a rummage sale. People are selling things they do not need or use. They are raising money for a new recreation center. You want to donate some old toys, but you are having a hard time parting with them.

   _____

   _____

Name: _____ Date: _____

Be a Helper

There are many helpers in your community. They might help other people. They might help animals. They might host activities. There are ways for you to be a helper, too.

Directions: List four things you have done to help others. Draw a star next to one of your ideas. Then, trace your hand in the box. Draw your idea inside your hand.

How I Have Helped Others

1. _____

2. _____

3. _____

4. _____

Name: _____ Date: _____

Good Leaders

No matter how big or small a community is, it needs good leaders. Leaders can be old or young. They can lead in a small town or a large city. They can be quiet or loud. But good leaders will have some qualities in common.

Focus on Community

Relationship Skills

Directions: Complete the web with qualities good leaders should have. Then, answer the questions.

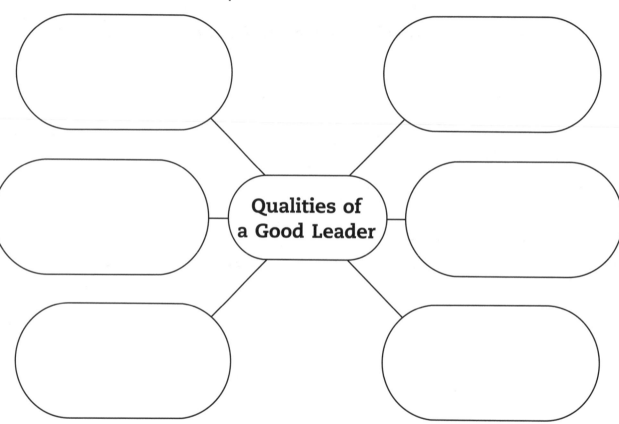

Qualities of a Good Leader

1. What leadership qualities do you have?

_____

2. How are you a leader?

_____

_____

126959—180 Days of Social-Emotional Learning

Name: _____ Date: _____

Plan to Solve Problems

It is helpful to plan ahead. It can help you avoid problems. But problems will always happen. Knowing how to solve them is an important skill.

Directions: Read the texts. Explain how Owen could solve each problem.

1. Owen is a student helper at his city's annual fair. He walks from booth to booth to make sure people have what they need. At the coffee counter, his neighbor Paul calls out, "Owen! We're out of to-go coffee cups! Can you help?"

   _____

   _____

2. Next, Owen goes to the farmers' market tables. He notices there is not enough room. Boxes of fruit are shoved under a table.

   _____

   _____

3. By evening, the band is getting ready to play. Owen hears the guitar player say they have not eaten dinner.

   _____

   _____

   _____

Focus on Community

Responsible Decision-Making

Name: _____ Date: _____

Focus on Self

Self-Awareness

Feelings and Actions

The way you think about yourself can shape how you act. Feeling good about yourself can lead you to do good things. Feeling bad about yourself can lead you to do bad things.

Directions: Read the scenario in the first box. Write how you would act in the second box.

1. You are getting ready to give a speech in front of your school.

You feel confident because you have practiced and feel ready.	_____ _____

You feel nervous because you have never had to speak in front of people.	_____ _____

2. A classmate did not invite you to a party at their house.

You feel angry because it wasn't nice to leave you out.	_____ _____

You don't mind because you already had plans with your family that night.	_____ _____

Name: _____ Date: _____

Relax Your Stress Away

When you are stressed, you might feel it in your whole body. Your muscles might feel tight, or your head might hurt. You might notice your fists or teeth are clenched. Progressive muscle relaxation can help. This means tensing and then relaxing your body one part at a time.

Directions: Practice the steps for progressive muscle relaxation. Then, answer the questions.

Face

1 Scrunch up your face, and hold for five seconds. Then, relax.

Shoulders

2 Bring your shoulders up to your ears, and hold for five seconds. Then, relax.

Hands

3 Squeeze your fists, and hold for five seconds. Then, relax.

Back

4 Arch your back, and push out your chest for five seconds. Then, relax.

Legs

5 Press your knees together, and hold for five seconds. Then, relax.

Toes

6 Curl your toes, and hold for five seconds. Then, relax.

1. Which step did you like best? Why?

_____

_____

2. How did you feel when you were finished with all the steps?

_____

_____

Focus on Self

Self-Management

Name: _____ Date: _____

Accept Gratitude

Think about something kind you did for someone else. They may have thanked you in some way. How did you respond? Sometimes, it's hard to know what to say or do when someone thanks you. But accepting gratitude is important to the person who gave it.

Directions: Answer the questions about gratitude.

1. Why can it be hard to accept gratitude?

_____

_____

2. Why should you accept someone's gratitude?

_____

_____

3. Draw one way you could accept gratitude from another person.

Name: _____ Date: _____

Communicate without Words

People use words to say what they mean. They can also do this without words. This is called *nonverbal communication*. It includes things such as facial expressions and body language. Listen to what people say. But also notice what they do not say. It will help you understand them better.

Directions: Write what you think each person is communicating.

1.

_____

2.

_____

3.

_____

4.

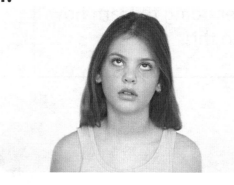

_____

Focus on Self

Relationship Skills

Name: _____ Date: _____

Overcome Your Fear of Failure

Trying new things is fun, but it can also be scary. People sometimes worry they will fail. You can try new things and overcome your fear of failure. Two things will help. You can focus on your effort and not your ability. You can also change your attitude to be more positive.

Directions: Imagine you want to do a cartwheel. Write positive things you could say to yourself to help.

Focus on Ability	Focus on Effort
I don't know how to do a cartwheel! My legs were bent, and I fell over.	

Negative Attitude	Positive Attitude
I'm not flexible and will probably hurt myself. I'm never going to learn how to do this.	

Name: _____ Date: _____

Show Integrity

Integrity is often explained as doing the right thing, even when no one is watching. It sounds simple. But it can be challenging. Having integrity builds trust with others. It makes you feel good about yourself. And it can even make the world a better place.

Directions: Write how you can show integrity in each situation. Then, describe a time you showed integrity.

1. You see the lid of your neighbor's recycling bin in the street.

   _____

   _____

2. You see a wallet on the trunk of a car at your friend's house. No one is around.

   _____

   _____

3. Mr. Sanchez has a big bucket of tennis balls on his sidewalk. Your dog loves to fetch tennis balls. Mr. Sanchez would never notice if just one was gone.

   _____

   _____

4. Describe a time you showed integrity.

   _____

   _____

Focus on Neighborhood

Self-Awareness

Name: _____ Date: _____

Use Self-Talk

Talking to yourself might feel strange, but it is a great way to manage your feelings! You can say kind and positive things to yourself. This can help you feel more confident.

Directions: Read the story. Then, answer the questions.

Goodbye, Toby

Toby and Chase have been best friends and next-door neighbors since they were four. But Toby's mom got a new job, and now his family is moving away. Toby knows he will miss Chase. He is also worried about starting at a new school. It is much larger than the one he goes to now. He loves the garden club at school, but doesn't know if his new school will even have one. Chase is feeling sad. He has never gone to school without Toby. Toby is so outgoing, and Chase is shy. He is worried it will be hard to fit in without his best friend.

1. What can Toby say to himself?

_____

_____

_____

2. What can Chase say to himself?

_____

_____

_____

Name: _____ **Date:** _____

Help in Hard Times

Sometimes, people go through hard times. They may have health problems. Maybe their families are going through changes. You can show concern and care for others. Think about how they might be feeling. Then, think of something you could do that might make them feel a little better. It doesn't have to be big or solve the problem. It just needs to show you care.

Directions: Write at least four ways you can show concern for others. Then, draw one item from your list.

Name: _____ Date: _____

Practice Teamwork

People often work together to finish a job. Teams share the work to help each other. Teamwork is best when everyone does their part. If someone does not help, the whole team feels the effects.

Directions: Read the text. Then, answer the questions.

The Lemonade Stand

You and two friends want to have a lemonade stand. There are a lot of items to get and tasks to finish before the stand can open. You want to make sure everyone does their part.

1. Write what each person should bring.

Name	Bring
_____	_____
_____	_____
_____	_____

2. Write what job each person should do.

Name	Job
_____	_____
_____	_____
_____	_____

Focus on Neighborhood

Relationship Skills

Name: _____ Date: _____

Know a Good Idea When You See It

People are full of ideas. Some ideas are good, but others might not be. It is important to know how to tell the difference. Good ideas can be safe, helpful, and fun.

Directions: Read the story. Then, answer the questions.

The Sledding Decision

After the big snow storm last night, all the kids in Tanvi's neighborhood are out sledding. Tanvi's yard has the best hill, and she loves having her friends at her house. They take turns zooming down the hill and throwing snowballs. After a while, Ben has an idea. He tells Tanvi and their friends they can go to his cousin's house. His cousin lives in a different neighborhood, but they can walk there. Ben says the hill is even bigger than Tanvi's! Everyone thinks it's a great idea. Tanvi isn't sure.

1. Do you think Ben has a good idea? Why or why not?

_____

_____

2. Draw the children doing what you think they should do.

Name: _____   Date: _____

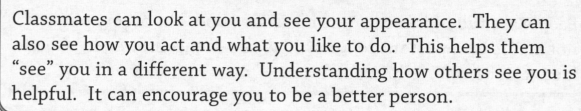

How Others See You

Classmates can look at you and see your appearance. They can also see how you act and what you like to do. This helps them "see" you in a different way. Understanding how others see you is helpful. It can encourage you to be a better person.

Directions: Complete the web with words that friends use to describe you.

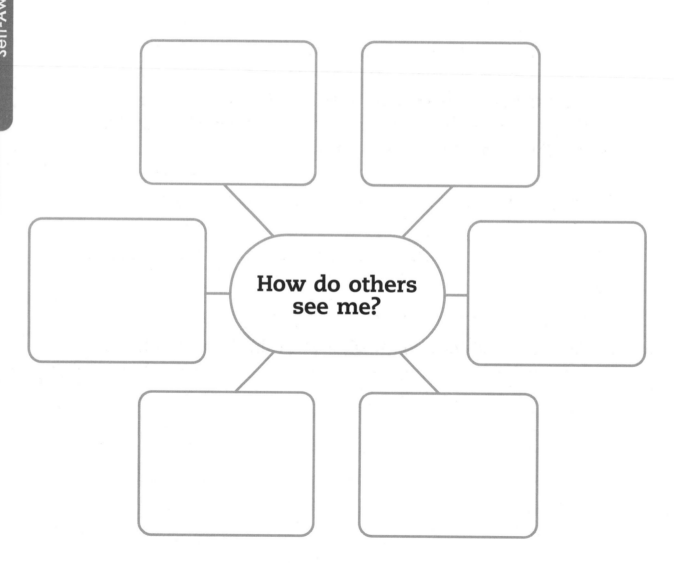

How do others see me?

Name: _____ Date: _____

Honesty and Integrity

Telling the truth in a tough situation is not always easy. But being honest is the right thing to do. It shows integrity.

Directions: Read the story. Then, answer the questions.

The Growing Library

Mr. Perez has a great classroom library. He lets his students borrow any of his books. Sura loves to read, but she doesn't have many books at home. She notices Mr. Perez often has two or three copies of the same books. Sura brings extra copies home in her backpack. She is happy because her bedroom library is growing!

1. Does Sura think she is doing something wrong? Explain your answer.

_____

_____

2. Do you think Sura is doing something wrong? Explain your answer.

_____

_____

3. What would you do if you saw Sura put a book in her backpack?

_____

_____

Focus on School

Self-Management

Name: _____   Date: _____

Different Rules in Different Schools

Students learn in different ways. They also learn in different places. Some students go to a big school with many classrooms. Some attend a small school. Others are homeschooled or learn online. All these schools might have different rules.

Directions: Circle two learning locations from the list, and write them on the lines. Complete a Venn diagram to compare and contrast the rules they might have. Write at least two ideas in each section.

big school	homeschool
small school	online school

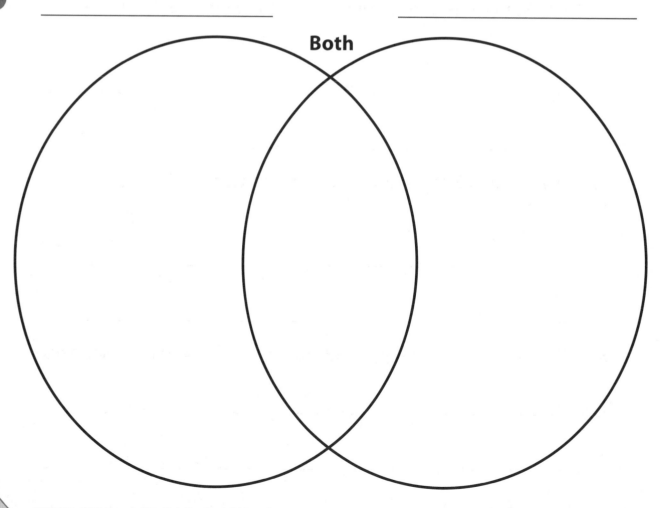

_____   _____

Both

© Shell Education

Focus on School

Social Awareness

Name: _____ Date: _____

Communicate Well

People who communicate well are good listeners. They are calm. They show respect. It takes practice to learn how to speak your mind in a respectful way.

Directions: Read the different ways people do not communicate well. Then, read the conflicts, and fill in the letters to show which type of poor communication is being used.

> **accusing**—blaming someone for doing something wrong
>
> **interrupting**—speaking while another person is still speaking
>
> **judging**—forming an opinion about someone or something
>
> **sarcasm**—saying the opposite of what you mean

Focus on School

Relationship Skills

1. "You were so smart when you said $4 + 2 = 10$."

   (A) accusing   (C) judging

   (B) interrupting   (D) sarcasm

2. "You were the one who left the window open when it rained."

   (A) accusing   (C) judging

   (B) interrupting   (D) sarcasm

3. "Your art project does not look good with those dark colors."

   (A) accusing   (C) judging

   (B) interrupting   (D) sarcasm

4. "I was just—" "You did not finish your homework!"

   (A) accusing   (C) judging

   (B) interrupting   (D) sarcasm

Name: _____ Date: _____

Listen for Solutions

People will not always agree. It is okay to disagree with someone. You can still be a good listener. You can find a solution, even if no one changes their minds.

Directions: Read the story. Then, draw a comic to show how the conflict could end.

Book Battle

Paulo and Jake are good friends. They both love to read. Paolo only reads nonfiction. He likes to learn facts and read about things that really happened. Jake only reads fiction. He loves fun stories and action. They are both reading books about dolphins. Paulo's book is about training dolphins. Jake's book is about a dolphin family that goes on a trip to the desert. Paulo tells Jake his book is silly. Jake tells Paulo his book is boring.

Name: _____ Date: _____

Contributions through the Seasons

A community needs help from the people who live there. It might have different needs at different times. Think about the times of year where you live. Does the weather change? Are there different activities? There may be different ways to help throughout the year.

Directions: Write one way to help your community in each season. Then, circle your favorite, and draw a picture of it.

Spring	**Fall**
_____ _____	_____ _____
Summer	**Winter**
_____ _____	_____ _____

Name: _____ Date: _____

Check Your List

Checklists are a great way to stay organized. They can list supplies you need to buy or chores you should finish. And crossing items off of a checklist is a great way to feel accomplished!

Directions: Imagine you are helping plan a party at your local park. Create two checklists to help the party go smoothly. One should list supplies you need to get. The other should list things you need to do to get the party area ready.

Supplies We Need

☐ _____   ☐ _____

☐ _____   ☐ _____

☐ _____   ☐ _____

Things to Do

☐ _____

☐ _____

☐ _____

Name: _____ Date: _____

Notice Needs

You might not always know when a person needs something. You can try to notice needs that are not obvious. You might be able to help. It might also mean telling an adult about the problem.

Directions: Answer the questions about the image.

Park Trail

Restroom

Focus on Community

Social Awareness

1. What needs do you notice in the dog park?

_____

_____

_____

2. How can you become better at noticing ways to help?

_____

_____

Name: _____ Date: _____

Communities of Fun

A community helps people who need it. People can also have fun together. They come together for events. They celebrate as a group. They make life better for each other all year long.

Directions: Read the story. Then, answer the questions.

Colt City Champs

The people of Colt City love the high school soccer team. Every year, fans attend all the games. But it has been years since the team made it to a championship game. Even when the team loses, the people of Colt City keep cheering. This year has been different, though. The team is playing great and made it all the way to the final game. The fans are excited and cheer loudly. Both teams play hard, but Colt City wins!

1. What do you think the Colt City community will do?

_____

_____

2. Draw what might happen next.

Name: _____ Date: _____

Your Community and You

Your community affects how you grow up. You might do different activities, go to school, and get to know different people in your community. But you can make a difference where you live, too. The choices you make can impact the people around you. You can choose to be kind. You can choose to follow the rules. You can choose to treat your community with respect.

Directions: Answer the questions.

1. What is something you like about your community?

   _____

   _____

2. What is something you wish was different about your community?

   _____

   _____

3. What choices can you make to improve your community?

   _____

   _____

   _____

Focus on Community

Responsible Decision-Making

Name: _____ **Date:** _____

Focus on Self

Self-Awareness

Emotion Synonyms

There can be a lot of ways to describe the same word. These are called *synonyms*. Emotions can have synonyms, too. The words may seem similar, but there are differences. Learning the right words for your emotions can help you understand your own feelings better.

Directions: Read the poem. Choose a different emotion, and write a poem about it using the same format.

Mad

by Kiley Smith

Angry

Frustrated

Irritated

Furious

Fuming

Cross

Mad is not the only word you can use.

Title: _____

by _____

_____

_____

_____

_____

_____

_____

_____ is not the only word you can use.

Name: _____ **Date:** _____

Goals Now and Later

Setting a goal is a great way to accomplish things. But not every goal takes the same amount of time. It takes a long time to learn a new language. It takes a lot less time to clean your room. Giving a goal a time frame helps you stay on task and gives you encouragement to finish.

Directions: Write a personal goal you can accomplish in each of the time frames. Then, draw yourself accomplishing one of your goals.

A goal I can accomplish...

today: _____

in a week: _____

in a month: _____

in a year: _____

Focus on Self

Self-Management

Name: _____ Date: _____

How Other People Feel

Your behavior can affect how other people feel. Both your good and bad actions can rub off on others. Knowing this can help you act in a positive way.

Focus on Self

Social Awareness

Directions: Explain how each person's behavior might affect the emotions of others.

1. Daniel laughed when he came into class. There was a substitute. Daniel was loud and silly all morning. He spoke when the teacher spoke. He threw little erasers at classmates.

   _____

   _____

2. Leja's family was going to eat dinner at a new restaurant. She didn't want to go. She sat in the car with her arms folded. When her parents shared some of the things on the menu, she rolled her eyes and sighed loudly.

   _____

   _____

3. Xavier was ready for art club. He arrived early and sat up front. He neatly set up his supplies. When the club leader spoke, Xavier smiled and nodded his head. He raised his hand when the leader asked questions.

   _____

   _____

Name: _____ Date: _____

Communicate Effectively

You check your understanding as you read. You can do the same thing when you communicate. Ask questions. Summarize what was said. This is also called *paraphrasing*. These steps will help you communicate more clearly.

Directions: Work with a partner through each part of a conversation. Use the tips below to guide you. Then, discuss whether the tips helped you and why or why not.

Relationship Skills

Focus on Self

Conversation Starters

- What is your favorite movie or TV show? Why?
- What do you like to do on the weekends?
- What is a funny memory you have?

Check for Understanding

- What did you mean by _____?
- Can you tell me more about _____?
- What else happened?

Paraphrasing Tips

You don't have to repeat exactly what your partner said.

If they told a story, share something from the beginning, middle, and end.

Say the most important or interesting things they shared.

Climb the Decision Tree

It can be hard to make decisions. There are often many options that seem like good choices. You can make better decisions by taking your time. Consider good and bad points of each choice.

Directions: Read the text. Complete the decision tree to help Logan decide what to do. Start at the bottom, and work up.

Friday Night

Logan is not sure what he should do Friday night. He has a basketball game. But his friend also invited him to watch a movie. He would like to do both things but can only do one.

Decision

| Good | Bad | Good | Bad |

Choice 1

Choice 2

What should I do on Friday?

Name: _____ **Date:** _____

Your Traits

Nobody is exactly the same as somebody else. Some people are cautious. Others are adventurous. Some people are outgoing. Others are shy. These traits are part of what makes you who you are. Your family can influence your traits. You might have some of the same traits as your family members.

Directions: Color the traits that describe you.

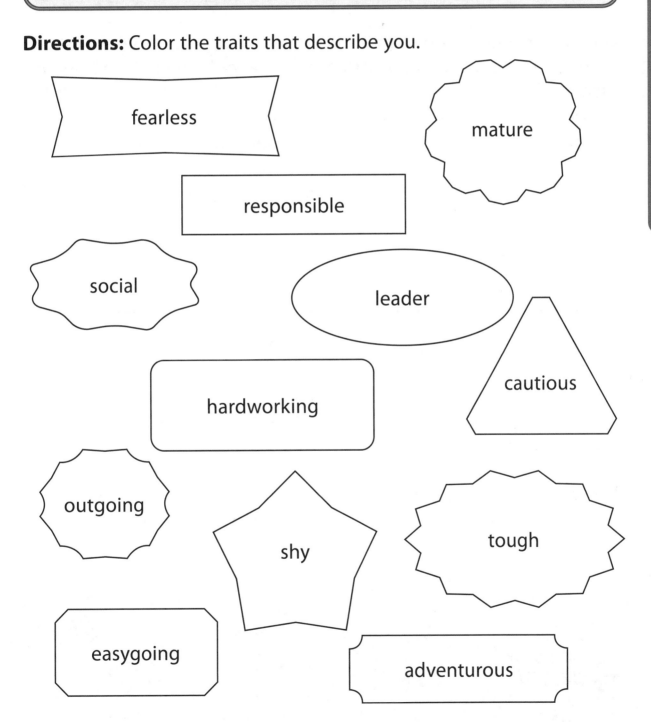

Name: _____ Date: _____

Try New Things

There are foods your family has eaten many times. They taste good and are probably some of your favorites. There are other foods you have never tried. Maybe you have never had a chance to eat them, or you just don't think they will taste good. But trying new foods can be a lot of fun.

Directions: Make a list of foods you like to eat. Then, make a list of foods you would like to try. Ask a friend or look online if you need ideas.

I like to eat...	I would like to try...
• _____	• _____
• _____	• _____
• _____	• _____
• _____	• _____
• _____	• _____

Directions: Ask your family if they would help you try one of the foods on your list! Maybe you will find a new family favorite.

Name: _____ **Date:** _____

Show Compassion

People in a family can help each other. They can show compassion. It can make a family stronger and closer. Doing something for your family members is a great way to show you care.

Directions: Put the name of a family member on each line. They do not need to be people who live in your home. Then, draw a kind thing you could do for them.

Focus on Family
Social Awareness

_____

_____

Name: _____ Date: _____

Resolving Conflicts Is a Win

Conflicts can be solved in many ways. One way is called Win-Lose. Only one person is happy with this type of solution. Another way is Lose-Lose. No one is happy with this solution. The third way is Win-Win. This means the problem is solved in a way that makes both people happy.

Focus on Family

Relationship skills

Directions: Read the story. Then, describe how Jack and Drew could solve the problem in the three different ways.

Bedroom Showdown

Jack and his brother Drew want to redecorate the room they share. Jack loves space and wants to paint stars on the walls. He thinks model rockets would look great on the shelves. Drew loves baseball. He wants to hang pictures of different stadiums on the walls. He thinks baseballs would look great on the shelves. The brothers cannot agree how their new room should look.

1. Win-Lose

_____

_____

2. Lose-Lose

_____

_____

3. Win-Win

_____

_____

126959—180 Days of Social-Emotional Learning   © Shell Education

Name: _____ Date: _____

Be a Mediator

It can be hard for two people to solve an argument. They might need help from another person. This person is called a *mediator*. A mediator listens to both sides. They help each person see the other's point of view. They help find solutions. They can help end an argument.

Directions: Read the beginning of the story. Then, write an ending that solves the problem.

Downed Drone

Kai saw his drone laying on the driveway in pieces and ran into the house. He saw his younger brother, Kenji, eating a snack at the table.

"Did you break my drone?" Kai asked.

Kenji shrugged and said, "You told me I could borrow it."

"I said you could borrow it, not break it!" Kai exclaimed. "What happened?"

Kenji explained that the drone hit the chimney and fell to the ground. Kai was furious. That drone was expensive! He knew Kenji didn't have enough money to replace it, and Kenji didn't even seem to care that he damaged the drone.

Kai knew he would need help to solve this conflict, so he went to find his dad to be a mediator.

_____

_____

_____

Name: _____ Date: _____

Focus on Friends

Self-Awareness

You Are Empowered

Speaking up for yourself is important. It can make you feel empowered, which means feeling strong and confident. It can be hard to speak up, but you will feel better when you do.

Directions: Read the situations. Then, answer the questions.

1. Joy and Tia like to play together after school. They have played basketball for the last week. It is Joy's favorite. Tia would rather play kickball. Today, Joy suggests basketball again. How can Tia speak up for herself?

   _____

   _____

2. Juan feels like his friend has been leaving him out lately. His friend is sitting at a different spot at lunch and not playing with him at recess. How can Juan speak up for himself?

   _____

   _____

3. Think of a time when you spoke up for yourself. Write about what happened.

   _____

   _____

   _____

126959—180 Days of Social-Emotional Learning   © Shell Education

Name: _____ Date: _____

Self-Talk for Self-Control

People don't always want to do what they know they should do. It takes self-control to finish tasks. If you feel like you need some self-control, try using positive self-talk. Remind yourself of what you need to do and why you need to do it.

Directions: The first frame of each comic shows a friend in a tough situation. Add self-talk in the second frame that would help.

1. Running a mile is so hard! There is no way we can finish.

2. This is my favorite show! We can finish our homework when it's over.

Focus on Friends

Self-Management

Name: _____ Date: _____

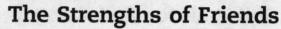

The Strengths of Friends

You and your friends have talents and strengths. You might have some that are the same and others that are different. Telling your friends what they are good at and what you admire about them is a great thing to do. It can help your friends feel confident and cared about.

Directions: List the strengths of two of your friends. Be sure to share your lists with each friend.

_____ is good at:
(Name)

- _____

- _____

- _____

_____ is good at:
(Name)

- _____

- _____

- _____

Name: _____ **Date:** _____

Decode Messages

When your friend speaks, what they say is just one part of their message. Their tone of voice also shows meaning. So does the look on their face. Decoding messages will help you communicate better.

Directions: Study each picture. Write how the person is feeling and how you know.

_____

_____

_____

_____

_____

_____

Directions: Draw what you look like when you feel excited.

Name: _____ Date: _____

Focus on Friends

Responsible Decision-Making

Make Amends

If a person does something wrong, they may say they are sorry. That is the right thing to do. But sometimes, there is more to be done. The person needs to make amends. That means that the person who is sorry will try to fix the problem.

Directions: Read the story. Then, answer the questions.

Mary's Painting

Mary wants to paint a field of flowers. Her friend, Gio, has a lot of painting supplies. Mary asks if she can borrow them. When Mary returns the supplies to Gio, he notices the brushes are clumped with dried paint. Mary forgot to rinse them when she finished painting. She tells Gio how sorry she is. He accepts her apology, but he still feels sad about his ruined brushes.

1. Draw how Mary could make amends to Gio.

2. Can people always make amends? Explain your answer.

_____

_____

_____

Name: _____ Date: _____

Intensity of Emotions

You would be happy if someone made your favorite meal. You would also be happy if you won a vacation. You would likely be happier about the vacation. The same emotion can have different intensity. This is how strong a feeling or thing is.

Directions: Write what emotion you would feel in each situation. Then, circle the number that matches how intensely you would feel the emotion.

3 = very intensely   2 = a medium amount   1 = just a little

1. Your school adds a week to spring break.

What emotion would you feel? _____

How intensely would you feel this emotion?   3   2   1

2. A power outage leaves your town without electricity.

What emotion would you feel? _____

How intensely would you feel this emotion?   3   2   1

3. Describe an event that happened in your community.

_____

What emotion did you feel? _____

How intensely did you feel this emotion?   3   2   1

Focus on Community   Self-Awareness

Name: _____ Date: _____

Strategies to Manage Stress

Being in a public place can be stressful for some people. They might feel crowded or nervous. If you ever feel that way, there are strategies you can use to help you feel calmer. Deep breathing is always a good choice. A hand massage is also a small and simple way you can lower your stress in public.

Directions: Follow the directions to give yourself a relaxing hand massage. Then, describe how you feel afterwards.

Step 1: Stretch your wrists by pointing your hands down and then up. Hold each position for three seconds.

Step 2: Lace your fingers together. Squeeze your hands for three seconds and then release.

Step 3: Use your pointer finger and thumb to gently squeeze the tip of your pinky finger. Then, squeeze the middle of your pinky and the bottom of your pinky. Repeat this for each finger on both hands.

Step 4: Press your thumb in a circle around your palms. Then, rub the middle of each palm with your thumb.

Step 5: Wiggle your fingers, and shake out your hands.

_____

_____

Name: _____ **Date:** _____

Send Gratitude in the Mail

It is nice to show gratitude if someone does something nice for you. You might tell them thank you. You could also send a card. Many people love to get mail. A simple note makes people feel appreciated.

Focus on Community

Social Awareness

Directions: Use the prompts to help you write a thank you note to someone. Then, create the note on another sheet of paper, decorate it, and give it to the person.

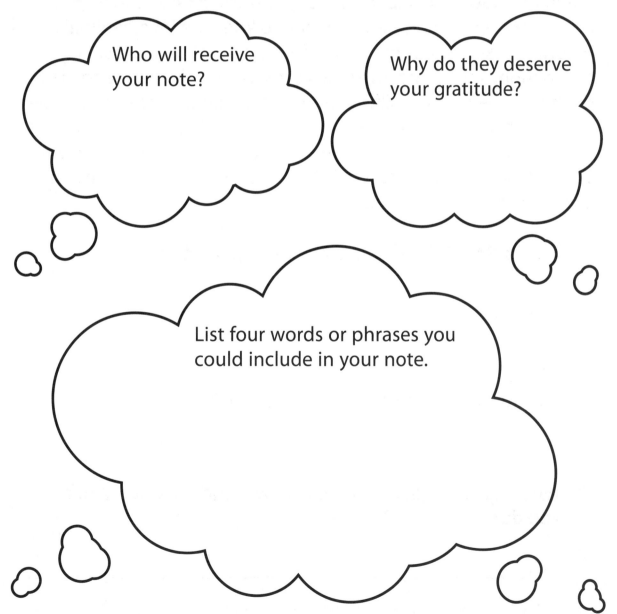

Who will receive your note?

Why do they deserve your gratitude?

List four words or phrases you could include in your note.

Name: _____ Date: _____

Focus on Community

Relationship Skills

Qualities of Good Leaders

Good leaders have a lot in common. They are responsible. They are organized. They care about people. Good leaders use all these things to make positive changes.

Directions: Read the story. Then, answer the questions.

Animal Lovers

Mr. Gilt was the leader of the city council in Zoe's town. Everyone knew who he was. They also knew he loved animals. He often talked to people about taking care of their pets. He raised money to create an animal preserve for the deer and elk in the area. Zoe saw Mr. Gilt helping at the animal shelter, too. Zoe loved animals. She wanted to get involved. She gathered towels and dog toys for the shelter. She donated some of her money to support the animal preserve. When Zoe saw Mr. Gilt in town, he always gave her a big smile.

1. How did Mr. Gilt influence Zoe to help animals?

   _____

   _____

2. Why do you think Mr. Gilt smiled at Zoe?

   _____

3. When have you been influenced by someone else? What did you do?

   _____

   _____

Problems and Solutions

Most problems have more than one solution. Every solution might solve the problem. But one is likely better than others. Think about all the solutions when you have a problem. Then, choose the best one.

Directions: Read the problem and the possible solutions. Then, answer the questions.

The Problem

Several hikers have been injured on the trails of a local park. Park officials know this is a problem. Something must be done to keep visitors safe. They came up with three solutions.

Solution 1	Solution 2	Solution 3
Close the trails to the public.	Pave the trails so they are concrete instead of dirt.	Require training before people can hike.

1. Which solution do you think is best? Why?

   _____

   _____

2. What problems might arise with the other solutions?

   _____

   _____

Focus on Community

Responsible Decision-Making

Name: _____ Date: _____

Honesty on the Internet

There is so much to do and so much to learn on the internet. You can show integrity online, too. Being honest online is important.

Directions: Read the story. Then, answer the questions.

Penguin Research

Hayden had a big report due in science. He had to research different types of penguins. Then, he had to write an essay to compare and contrast them. Hayden found a great site on the internet. He wrote a few notes. As he scrolled down on the webpage, his eyes grew wide. There was a chart comparing and contrasting the two types of penguins he had chosen. Hayden copied the chart into his notes. This would be perfect in his essay.

1. Do you think Hayden should copy the chart into his essay? Why or why not?

   _____

   _____

2. If you were Hayden, what would you do with the chart?

   _____

   _____

3. What does it mean to be honest online?

   _____

   _____

Focus on Self

Self-Awareness

Name: _____ **Date:** _____

Self-Discipline Online

Being online can be a lot of fun. There are games to play, things to read, and information to learn. But being online too much can be a bad thing. Studies show that some children spend four to six hours a day on screens. That includes tablets, phones, TVs, and computers. Being online is great. But it's also important to do other things. This takes self-discipline.

Directions: Answer the question. Then, draw four things you can do instead of being on a screen.

1. What might happen if you spend too much time on the internet?

_____

_____

Self-Management · Focus on Self

Name: _____ Date: _____

Focus on Self

Social Awareness

The Rules of the Web

A home, a school, and a store all have rules. Some may be the same, but others are different. The internet has rules, too. Many of those rules help keep you safe. Others remind people to be kind. Following internet rules will make your time online more fun.

Directions: Make a list of five rules to keep people safe when they are online.

Internet Safety Rules

1. _____

   _____

2. _____

   _____

3. _____

   _____

4. _____

   _____

5. _____

   _____

Name: _____ Date: _____

Computer Communication

Writing letters used to be common. It was how people communicated. Now, we have computers. We write emails. We send messages. We use emojis and abbreviations. Knowing what these mean can be helpful.

Focus on Self

Relationship Skills

Directions: Write what each abbreviation means. Check with a friend if you are not sure.

1. LOL _____

2. BTW _____

3. FYI _____

4. IDK _____

Directions: Write the letter of the emoji that represents the text.

A   **B**   **C**   **D**

5. _____ I agree

6. _____ congratulations

7. _____ so sad

8. _____ surprised

Name: _____ Date: _____

How to Judge Websites

People often use the internet for research. There is a lot of information online. It is fast and easy to find. But not everything on the internet is true. You need to learn how to judge whether a website is credible. That means it is trustworthy and has good facts.

Directions: Study the table. Underline the important information. Then, answer the questions.

Questions	Reason
What type of website is it?	The end of a website can give hints about its purpose. For example, government (.gov) and education (.edu) sites are meant to inform.
Who wrote the article?	Make sure the author knows about the article's topic. For example, if the article is about a sickness, it is good if the author is a doctor.
When was the article written?	An article that is several years old may not be good to use. The information may be out of date.
Does it look like a credible site?	It isn't always possible to tell just by looking at a site. But if it has lots of ads and pop-ups or spelling mistakes, be careful.

1. What other questions might you consider about a website?

_____

_____

_____

Name: _____ Date: _____

Core Values and Choices

Everyone has core values. These are the basic beliefs that guide you in your life. Honesty and respect are common core values. So are service and being responsible. Your faith can be another core value. Knowing your own core values will help you make good choices.

Directions: Answer the questions about your core values.

1. When have you shown the core value of respect?

   _____

   _____

2. How have you shown the core value of service?

   _____

   _____

3. What core value is most important to you? Why?

   _____

   _____

   _____

Name: _____ Date: _____

Planning to Help Others

There are many ways to help others. Some are quick and simple. Others take more time and planning. Helping neighbors and people you know can make your neighborhood a better place.

Directions: Complete the chart to make a plan to help a neighbor. Then, use your plan to help them.

Who will you help?	
What will you do?	
When will you help them?	
What supplies will you need?	
Are there any special instructions? If so, what?	

Name: _____ Date: _____

Read Body Language

A person's body language can help you predict their mood. Imagine watching a person walk down your street. How would they walk if they were sad? What about if they were happy? How do someone's shoulders look when they are scared? When they are confident? Body language can help you better understand others.

Directions: Take turns acting out and guessing each emotion with a partner. Then, answer the questions.

angry	excited
bored	scared
embarrassed	surprised

1. Which was your favorite emotion to act out? Why?

   _____

   _____

2. How can noticing body language help you be a better neighbor?

   _____

   _____

Name: _____ Date: _____

Positive Neighbor Relationships

It is good to have positive relationships with your neighbors. They can be there if you need help. They can be friends in good times and bad times. You can teach and take care of each other.

Directions: Read the story. Then, answer the questions.

Miss McGee

Miss McGee is Tasha's neighbor. They live across the hall from each other on the third floor. Every day after school, Tasha goes to Miss McGee's apartment until her mom gets home from work. Miss McGee can't see very well anymore. Tasha reads the news to her. Miss McGee can still bake, though! She always has cookies or fresh bread waiting on the table when Tasha arrives. Most days, she also shows Tasha how to make some of her favorite recipes. Tasha washes the dishes and sweeps the floor after Miss McGee is finished in the kitchen. Miss McGee and Tasha both know they are loved.

1. How do Tasha and Miss McGee help each other?

_____

_____

_____

2. What do Tasha and Miss McGee learn from each other?

_____

_____

Name: _____ Date: _____

Stay Curious

Trying new things can be fun. You might discover a new talent or a hobby. You might learn you don't really like something. You might even find new ideas for future jobs. Being curious will help you learn new things about yourself.

Directions: Study the flyer about a career fair in the neighborhood. Then, rank the activities based on how much you want to do each one. Write *5* next to the one you want to do most, and continue down to *1* next to the one you want to do least.

_____ bake   _____ make a birdhouse

_____ paint   _____ train a dog

_____ learn to code

Focus on Neighborhood

Responsible Decision-Making

Name: _____ Date: _____

Focus on School

Self-Awareness

Learn More to Feel Better

There are so many subjects to learn about. Learning new things can help you discover new interests. This can lead to new skills and new hobbies. This knowledge can make you feel confident!

Directions: Circle the subjects you would like to learn about. Add three topics to the list. Then, draw your favorite.

animals	history	sports
cooking	instruments	swimming
crafts	maps	technology
drawing	oceans	writing stories
electronics	other countries	_____
geometry	outer space	_____
gymnastics	problem-solving	
health	sewing	_____
hiking	singing	

Name: _____ Date: _____

Plan to Stay Organized

People often use calendars and checklists to keep their lives organized. Students may use homework planners. This reminds them about assignments they have to do. They might add test dates or when projects are due. Learning to keep a planner will help you as you get older, too.

Directions: Study this page from Theo's homework planner. Then, answer the questions.

	Monday	**Tuesday**	**Wednesday**	**Thursday**	**Friday**
Reading		read Chapter 5		turn in vocabulary	
Math	homework due		math test		
Science		bring rock			
Social Studies		turn in worksheet			test

1. When does Theo have to turn in math homework?

   _____

2. On what two days does Theo have reading work due?

   _____

   _____

3. What should Theo do for social studies on Thursday?

   _____

4. Do you use a planner? Why or why not?

   _____

   _____

Focus on School

Self-Management

Name: _____ Date: _____

Learn from All Your Teachers

Students learn things from teachers. But teachers are not the only ones who teach. You have likely learned lessons from many people in your life. They may have taught you about a subject they know a lot about. They may have shared life experiences. Noticing what other people are good at helps them feel special and can teach you a lot.

Directions: Make a list of people who have taught you something. Then, write what you learned. The list below can help you get started.

babysitter	neighbor
coach	relative
friend	religious leader
music teacher	tutor

1. _____ _____

   _____

2. _____ _____

   _____

3. _____ _____

   _____

Name: _____ **Date:** _____

Communication Street

Communication is a two-way street. The sender wants to make sure the message is clear. They need feedback from the receiver. The receiver might nod or smile if they understand. But if they do not understand the message, then they might shake their head or frown. This feedback helps both people communicate.

Directions: Draw two pictures of two people communicating. In the first one, show that the receiver understands the sender. In the second, show that the receiver does not understand the sender.

Name: _____ Date: _____

Cause and Effect of Conflict

Conflicts are common. One way you can help solve a conflict is to figure out the cause and effect. The cause is the reason the conflict happened. The effect is the result. Knowing these things can help you see the problem more clearly. Then, you can think about solutions.

Directions: Read the story. Then, answer the questions.

President Battle

Corey and Eric both love to learn. They thought it would be fun to research presidents. Corey thought George Washington was the best. Eric thought Abraham Lincoln was better. Both boys checked out books about the presidents they admired most. They learned a lot about their favorites. One day during lunch, they began arguing about which president was better. Corey moved to a different table to eat. Eric decided to not talk to Corey. Their teacher noticed the problem and wanted to help.

1. What was the cause of the conflict?

   _____

2. What was the effect of the conflict?

   _____

3. If you were the teacher, how would you help solve the conflict?

   _____

   _____

Name: _____ **Date:** _____

What's Your Role?

There are many different roles in a community. But everyone is part of where they live, work, learn, and play. You have a role, too. And as you get older, your role will grow and may change. You can choose how you are involved in your community.

Directions: Study the list of ways to help your community. Then, answer the questions.

caregiver	teacher
helper	volunteer
leader	worker

1. What would you like to do in your community now?

   _____

   _____

2. Draw how your role might change when you are older.

Name: _____ Date: _____

Focus on Community

Self-Management

"I" Can Stay Calm

I-messages are a good way to manage your emotions. When you are in a conflict, they can help you stay calm. They can help the other person feel like you are not blaming them. They can help you share your feelings.

Directions: Read the skit. Then, answer the questions.

Setting: A town council meeting. Tomás and Mark are arguing about putting a traffic light at an intersection.

Tomás: The intersection of Elm Street and Maple Drive is not safe! There is too much traffic. I feel like it would be safer to have a traffic light at the intersection.

Mark: You are wrong. You don't drive on those streets often. I live on Maple Drive and do not want a traffic light there. Having a traffic light will mean people will sit and wait their turn. It will take me longer to get to work.

Tomás: I hear what you are saying. And I understand you are frustrated. It might take extra time to wait at the light. But it is worth it if it means there are fewer accidents.

Mark: I didn't think about fewer accidents. Maybe the traffic light is a good idea.

1. Circle the I-messages in the skit. Who is using more I-messages?

   _____

2. What effect did the I-messages have?

   _____

   _____

Name: _____ Date: _____

Observe to Understand

No one can read minds, but you can observe others in a situation. You can predict how others feel based on what they are going through. Understanding how others feel is kind. It helps you have empathy.

Directions: Answer the questions about how others feel.

1. Tessa ran for mayor of her small town. She won the election. How do you think Tessa feels? Why?

   _____

   _____

2. Carrie trained for her city's summer marathon. The day before the race, she twisted her ankle. How do you think Carrie feels? Why?

   _____

   _____

3. Ian's dog jumped over the fence and has been lost for over a week. His neighbor just called and said he found the dog. How do you think Ian feels? Why?

   _____

   _____

   _____

© Shell Education

Focus on Community

Social Awareness

Name: _____ Date: _____

Appreciate Different Cultures

Some communities have a lot of different cultures. In other areas, a lot of people from one culture live in the same place. All cultures have things to teach. Learning about cultures can help you understand others. It can help you be more open-minded.

Directions: Read the text. Then, draw what the Lunar New Year celebration might look like.

Lunar New Year

Mei's community is getting ready. The Lunar New Year will begin tomorrow. To prepare, everyone cleans their houses to get rid of last year's bad luck. They fill red envelopes with money to give to others.

The festivities start with the dragon dance. Mei loves to watch the people make their way down the street as a dragon. She can't wait to give gifts and watch fireworks. Her family will wear plenty of red. It is the color of luck, after all!

The celebrations will last for 15 days. A lantern ceremony takes place on the last night. Mei loves to watch the night sky light up with the glowing lanterns.

Focus on Community

Relationship Skills

Healthy Communities

People try to stay healthy. Some people exercise. Others try to eat healthy foods. Communities can also try to be healthy. But different things keep them healthy. You can reflect on how your community is doing. There might be a way you can make it better.

Directions: Study the web. Then, answer the questions.

```
        is safe.                          has good
                                          schools.

has jobs                 A healthy                  has hospitals
and homes for            community...               and doctors.
people.

   has places                           has public
   for outdoor                          transportation.
   activities.
```

1. How is your community healthy?

_____

_____

2. How could your community be even better?

_____

_____

Name: _____ **Date:** _____

The Strength of Tradition

A person's culture includes many things. Your traditions and the way you dress can be part of your culture. So can the holidays you observe and the way you talk. A religion might also be part of your culture. These things are all assets. They make a place stronger.

Directions: Draw one of your culture's traditions.

Name: _____ Date: _____

Show Your Feelings

Emotions can be shown or explained in many ways. Poems can share feelings. A poem about sunshine might show happiness. A poem about fire might show anger. Poems about feelings can sometimes show what is hard to say.

Directions: Read the poem. Then, answer the questions.

The Storm

Lightning fills the sky.
Thunder cracks in the distance.
Wind whips at the building.

Rain cascades on the window panes.
Lights flicker.
Trees quake and quiver.

The storm is here.
Will it ever leave?

1. What emotion does this poem make you feel? Why?

_____

_____

2. What emotion are you feeling today?

_____

3. On a separate sheet of paper, write a short poem showing that emotion.

Name: _____ Date: _____

Focus on Self

Social Awareness

Helping a Sad Friend

Everyone feels sad sometimes. One day, you might notice that a friend is sad. You can show you care by showing concern for their feelings. Talking to your friend might help them. Just being with them can also help.

Directions: Work with a partner. One of you should pretend to be sad. The other should work through these steps to help. Switch parts and do it again. Then, answer the questions.

Approach Your Friend Tell your friend what you observe. You might say, "It looks like you're sad."
Ask Your Friend a Question Ask how your friend is feeling or if they want to talk. You might say, "Is everything okay? Is there anything you want to talk about?"
Keep the Attention on Your Friend Be a good listener. This is not the time to talk about yourself.

1. How did it feel to be the friend who was sad? How did your friend help?

   _____

   _____

2. How did it feel to be the friend who helped?

   _____

   _____

Name: _____ Date: _____

Know Your Bias

A *bias* is leaning a certain way in your thinking. You might like or dislike an idea or item. All people have a bias toward or against things. Imagine your whole family loves a sports team. You have a bias for that team. Maybe a type of candy once made you sick. You might have a bias against it. A bias can affect the way you get along with others.

Directions: Read the story. Then, answer the questions.

Beach Day

Sanjay is excited. He is headed to the beach for the first time. Mr. and Mrs. Cook are taking him with their children, Ari and Bella.

"Every time we go to the beach, I get sunburned," Ari tells Sanjay. "No matter how much sunscreen I put on, I always burn. It's sore and then itchy for days."

"I always make sand castles," Bella says. "We have buckets that are different shapes. They help us make super cool castles."

Sanjay hadn't thought about sunburns or sand castles. There are a lot of things that can happen at the beach.

1. What is Ari's bias about the beach? How do you know?

_____

_____

2. What is Bella's bias about the beach? How do you know?

_____

_____

Name: _____ Date: _____

Kindness Ripples

Actions can be like ripples in a pond. They touch others and get bigger the farther away they get. Little acts of kindness can also affect others. Look for ways to be kind. No matter how small they seem, they can make a big difference.

Directions: Write the effect kindness might have in each situation.

1. Your favorite sweatshirt is too small now. You give it to your younger sibling.

   _____

   _____

2. As you're walking down the street, you see a cup on the sidewalk. You pick it up and throw it away.

   _____

   _____

3. Your friend is struggling with math. You help him study and practice his math facts.

   _____

   _____

4. Your grandma gives you money for your birthday. You decide to donate half of it to your city's food pantry.

   _____

   _____

Name: _____ Date: _____

Try New Things Together

Neighbors often do things as a group. They might enjoy trying new things. It might be a class or a hobby. It might be something one person teaches another. Learning something new with others can be fun. You are all trying together.

Directions: Complete the web with things neighbors can try together. Then, answer the question.

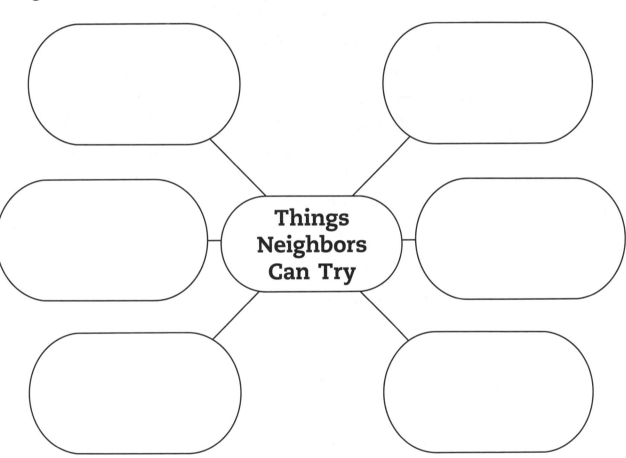

Things Neighbors Can Try

1. What new thing would you like to try in your neighborhood? Why?

_____

_____

Name: _____ **Date:** _____

Neighborhood Goals

People often set goals. Neighborhoods can set them, too. They might have a meeting to talk about any problems. They can brainstorm how to solve them. They can talk about goals and plan how they can achieve them. Setting a goal gives people a chance to work together.

Directions: Read the story. Then, answer the questions.

The Busy Bees

Sally's neighborhood is busy. Her building is 20 stories high. People are always coming and going. Most of the parents have full-time jobs. Most of Sally's friends are involved in an activity or sport. Plus, all her friends have school and homework. The grandparents in the building get together to play cards. Even the pets seem to have places to be.

"You know, I don't think we have had a community gathering in months," Sally said one morning.

"You're right," her grandma said sadly. "Something needs to change!"

1. What goal could the neighbors set?

   _____

   _____

2. How can they meet their goal?

   _____

   _____

Neighborhood Rules

All neighborhoods have rules. But they are not all the same. One group of people might think another's rules are unfair or not needed. Neighborhoods have different needs and rules to match.

Directions: Answer the questions about this neighborhood's rules.

Longwood Neighborhood Rules

No picnics allowed.

Pick up after your dog.

Don't park on side streets.

Obey all speed limits.

No loud phone conversations.

1. Which rules do you think are fair? Why?

_____

_____

2. Do you think any rules are unfair? Why or why not?

_____

_____

Name: _____ **Date:** _____

Teamwork with Neighbors

Every neighborhood has problems. But people can work together as a team. They can think of ways to solve the problem. They can help each other. Practicing teamwork with neighbors can be fun. And it will make things easier for everyone.

Focus on Neighborhood

Relationship Skills

Directions: Read the text. Then, draw how the neighborhood can work together while the family is gone.

An Empty House

Imagine a street with several homes and families. The mom in one family just got a new job. She has to train for her job in another town. The entire family will be gone for one week. Their house will be empty.

Name: _____ **Date:** _____

Reflect on Your Neighbors

To reflect is to think deeply about a topic. You can reflect on your friendships. You can reflect on a problem. You can even reflect on a hobby. Reflecting helps you understand things better. It can organize your thoughts. It is time well spent.

Directions: Reflect on what it means to be a good neighbor. Then, answer the questions.

1. What is important in a neighborhood?

_____

_____

_____

2. What should a neighborhood do?

_____

_____

_____

3. How can neighbors help one another?

_____

_____

_____

Name: _____ Date: _____

The Chain of Feelings

Your feelings are impacted by events in your life. One thing can cause another to happen. An event might cause an action. Then, that action makes you feel a certain way. This is called a *chain reaction*.

Directions: Complete each chain by writing how you might feel in the situation.

1.

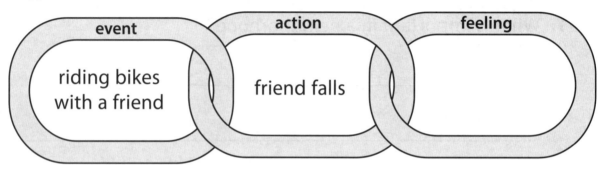

event: riding bikes with a friend

action: friend falls

feeling:

2.

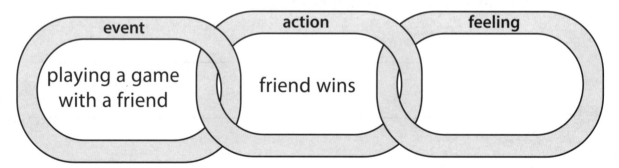

event: playing a game with a friend

action: friend wins

feeling:

3. Create your own chain reaction.

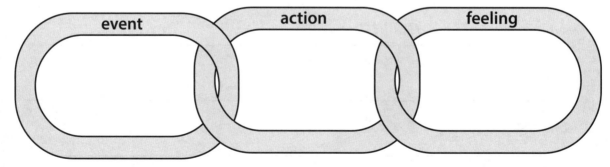

event

action

feeling

Name: _____ Date: _____

Learn How to Help Others

Sometimes, helping friends is easy. If they lose a pencil, you can loan them one of yours. Sometimes, helping is harder. It might take time or even sacrifice. You might not be able to help on your own. It is good to learn how to help your friends.

Directions: Draw a time you helped a friend. Then, explain your drawing in at least two sentences.

_____

_____

_____

Name: _____ Date: _____

Another Perspective

You and a friend might be together and have the same experience. But you might not react to it the same way. You might remember it differently. You might have different feelings about it. Part of being a good friend is seeing things from your friend's perspective.

Directions: Read the story. Then, answer the questions.

The New Video Game

Kenzie invited Liz to come over after school and play her new video game. Liz had never been to Kenzie's before. She really wanted to try the new game, too. Liz was excited.

Kenzie and Liz had been playing for a half hour when the doorbell rang. Kenzie went to answer it. A few moments later, she came back with another girl from their class, Josie.

"Josie lives down the street," Kenzie explained. "She stopped by, and I invited her to play with us."

Liz felt angry. She didn't want Josie to play with them. Kenzie didn't think it was a big deal.

1. Why do you think Liz is angry?

_____

_____

2. Why does Kenzie think it was no big deal?

_____

_____

Name: _____ **Date:** _____

Stand Up to Peer Pressure

Having friends is a wonderful thing. You can have fun together and support each other. But sometimes, a friend might pressure you to do something you should not. This is called *peer pressure*. It can be hard to stand up to peer pressure, but doing the right thing is worth it.

Directions: Read the text. Then, answer the question.

The Sleepover

Imagine you are sleeping over at a friend's house. After dinner, you decide to watch a movie. Your friend chooses a movie you are not allowed to see. It has a lot of violence. You tell your friend, but they say it will be fine and that your family will never know you watched it. You don't know what to do. You know you shouldn't watch the movie, but your friend really seems to want to.

1. What would you say to your friend? Why? Use one of the examples below, or write your own.

_____

_____

What You Could Say

- I don't like movies like this. Let's choose something else.
- I know my family would find out. And then I'd be in trouble.
- It feels wrong to lie about watching the movie. I'd rather watch something else.
- I don't want to watch a movie. Let's play games instead.

Focus on Friends

Relationship Skills

Name: _____ Date: _____

Impacts of Friendship

Friendships are an important part of life. You can have fun with friends, and you can support each other. Thinking about how your friends have impacted your life can be helpful. It can make you a better friend and help you realize who your good friends are.

Directions: Answer the questions about your friends.

1. What is a special memory you have with a friend?

   _____

   _____

2. When has a friend cheered you up or comforted you?

   _____

   _____

3. When have you been a good friend to someone else?

   _____

   _____

4. What do you think makes someone a good friend?

   _____

   _____

Focus on Friends

Responsible Decision-Making

Name: _____ Date: _____

Prejudice

Prejudice is when someone doesn't like a person or group for unfair reasons. People can feel this way because of someone's skin color, gender, religion, or because of how rich or poor someone is. It could be about where a person lives. All people should be treated with fairness and kindness. Prejudice is wrong.

Directions: Answer the questions about prejudice.

1. Have you ever seen prejudice in your community? Explain your answer.

_____

_____

_____

2. Why is prejudice wrong?

_____

_____

3. How can people help stop prejudice?

_____

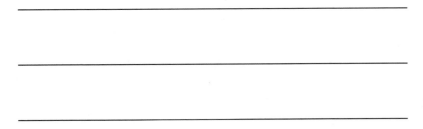

_____

_____

Focus on Community

Self-Awareness

Name: _____ Date: _____

Community Goals

People want their communities to be good places to live. They might work together to make this happen. Setting a goal is a smart place to start. Then, the people know what they are trying to accomplish. A goal for a community is big. But when everyone does their part, they can meet the goal.

Directions: Read about a community's goal. Then, create a flyer for the bake sale. Be sure to include what the event is and how the money will be used. Mention where and when the bake sale will happen.

Wildlife Preserve

Lakeville is a small community. It used to be surrounded by woods. Now, new neighborhoods are popping up. The people in Lakeville want to make a wildlife preserve. It will help keep the wildlife safe. They need $1,000 to get it started. They plan to hold fundraisers. One of the fundraisers is a bake sale. It will be held Saturday afternoon in the school gym.

Name: _____ **Date:** _____

Strengths in Others

Your community is filled with people. They have different jobs and ways they help others. They have different talents and skills. This helps make a community stronger. Noticing others' strengths helps you feel thankful.

Directions: Write a strength or skill of each community worker.

Community Worker	Strength or Skill
teacher	
mayor	
police officer	
doctor	
banker	
trash collector	

Name: _____ Date: _____

Focus on Community

Relationship Skills

Help When Needed

People often like to finish work themselves. It makes them feel capable. They might also feel proud. But everyone needs help sometimes. Knowing when and how to ask for help is a good skill to have.

Directions: Read the story. Then, answer the questions.

Mr. Miller's Garden

Mr. Miller is a kind, old man. He has been in charge of the city garden for many years. He teaches children to grow peppers and carrots and helps adults pull weeds from their plots. Lately, though, the work has made him tired. His knees and back hurt after a day in the garden. He thinks it is time for him to step down from being in charge of the garden. He doesn't like to admit it, but he needs help.

1. Why does Mr. Miller need help?

_____

2. How could Mr. Miller ask for help? Give at least two suggestions.

_____

_____

3. When did you need to ask for help? How did you do it?

_____

_____

Name: _____ Date: _____

Make Big Decisions

People make hundreds of decisions every day. Some are easy. Others are harder and need to be thought about carefully. If you have a big choice to make, you should learn about all the facts. That can help you make a wise decision.

Directions: A city wants to build a walking bridge over a local creek. Two different companies want to build it. They each shared facts about their business and the scope of the project. Use the information in the chart to answer the question.

	Company A	**Company B**
Online review	★★★☆☆	★★★★☆
Cost for project	$1,300	$1,500
Number of workers	5	7
Time to complete	8 days	5 days

1. Should the city choose Company A or B? Why?

_____

_____

_____

_____

Name: _____ Date: _____

Have a Growth Mindset

A growth mindset means you know you can get better at something. Time, practice, and hard work can help you improve. Sometimes, you are already good at something. That is great, but that doesn't have to be the end of that skill. Having a growth mindset means you can get even better.

Directions: List three things you do well. They could be related to sports, school, hobbies, or feelings. Then, write something you can do to become even better at each thing.

1. _____

How can you become even better?

_____

_____

2. _____

How can you become even better?

_____

_____

3. _____

How can you become even better?

_____

_____

Move the Stress Away

It is normal to feel stress sometimes. But it's important to know how to help yourself when you feel stressed. Deep breathing and relaxing can help. Exercising and moving your body can also be a great stress reliever. And it's fun, too.

Directions: Create a short exercise routine. Be sure to say how many times to do each exercise. Then, practice your routine, and draw yourself doing your favorite exercise.

Exercise Routine

1. _____

2. _____

3. _____

4. _____

5. _____

Name: _____ Date: _____

You Deserve Self-Compassion

People are kind to their friends. But sometimes, people are not kind to themselves. They blame themselves or are hard on themselves. Showing self-compassion means being nice to yourself. You deserve it.

Directions: Read the story. Then, answer the questions.

The Forgotten Spelling Test

Cade's week was very busy. He had homework every night and swim practice twice. It was also his week to walk the dog.

"I'm so glad it's finally Friday!" he told his friend Hao as they walked into class after lunch.

"Me too," Hao replied. "Once this spelling test is over, the rest of the day will go quickly."

"The spelling test!" Cade exclaimed. "I forgot all about it. I didn't study at all. I can't believe I missed this!"

1. Why is Cade upset?

_____

2. How could Cade show self-compassion?

_____

_____

3. Think about a time you made a mistake. How could you have shown self-compassion?

_____

_____

Name: _____ **Date:** _____

Following the Leader

Leaders can change the way people feel. If a leader is kind and patient, people may feel confident. If a leader is bossy or mean, people may feel sad and stressed. What leaders do and say to others matters.

Directions: Write what you would say in response to each conversation.

1.

I do not understand what we are learning in math.

2.

I feel lonely at recess every day.

3. My mom is coming home tomorrow. She was serving in the military for a whole year.

4.

I'd like to be a part of the community service club.

Name: _____ Date: _____

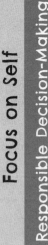

Work for the Boss

At some point in your life, you will have a boss. It might be when you are an adult with a job or when you are a child and do work for a neighbor. Your boss will want you to be able to solve problems. Thinking of solutions and carrying them out will make you a better worker.

Directions: Read the story. Then, complete the table.

Pet-Sitting Problems

Aisha was excited. Her neighbors were going on vacation, and Aisha was going to take care of their dog. She had to check on him three times a day and make sure he had food and water. She also had to take him on a walk every morning and night.

The first day did not go as expected! Aisha could not find the dog's leash anywhere. He had spilled his water all over the floor, and the dog food bag was almost empty. Aisha had some problems to fix.

What problems did Aisha have?	How could she solve them?
1.	
2.	
3.	

Name: _____ **Date:** _____

Know Yourself

People see themselves a certain way. They may think they are kind or shy or impatient. It's good to know yourself. It is also important to know how others see you. You can learn if your actions match your true self.

Directions: Answer the first question about yourself. Then, ask the second question to a neighbor, and write their answer. If you can't talk to a neighbor, write what you think they would say. Then, answer the third question.

1. How would you describe yourself? (Answer about yourself.)

    _____

    _____

    _____

2. How would you describe me? (Ask a neighbor.)

    _____

    _____

    _____

3. Do you think others see you as you see yourself? Why or why not?

    _____

    _____

    _____

Name: _____ Date: _____

Focus on Neighborhood

Self-Management

Be Scared and Brave

Being brave does not mean a person isn't scared. A brave person does something even if it is a little scary. Trying new things can be tough. Try to overcome your fears so they don't stop you from trying something new.

Directions: Read the story. Then, answer the questions.

Saying Hello

Katya wanted to run outside and introduce herself to the new girl who just moved in next door. Maybe they could be friends. But she felt so nervous. What would she say? What if the girl didn't like her? What if they didn't have anything in common?

There was only one way to find out the answer to her questions. Katya took a deep breath and went outside to say hello.

1. What was Katya's fear?

_____

2. What did Katya do about her fear?

_____

3. Draw what might happen next.

Name: _____ **Date:** _____

Notice How Others Feel

People in the same situation can feel different things. Thinking about how a person feels will help you be more aware. You can treat people in a way that makes sense. You wouldn't say the same thing to a sad person as you would to a happy person.

Directions: Read the text. Then, write how each person might feel about the new school year and why you think so.

New School Year

A neighborhood is having a party. Teachers, students, and parents are celebrating the start of a new school year. Almost all the neighbors are there. They are eating snacks, listening to music, and talking with each other. But they don't all feel the same way about a new school year.

1. teacher _____

_____

2. third-grader _____

_____

3. parent _____

_____

4. kindergartner _____

_____

Name: _____ Date: _____

Communicating without Words

Think about walking down the street. You see a neighbor. There are many ways you could communicate without using words. Gestures can get your message across. So can body language.

Directions: Describe how you could communicate each sentence without using words. Then, try it out with a partner.

1. "Hi!" _____

_____

2. "I don't know." _____

_____

3. "It's hot." _____

_____

4. "It's cold." _____

_____

5. "What time is it?" _____

_____

Name: _____ Date: _____

Big and Small Problems in the Neighborhood

All neighborhoods have problems. There might be an argument between two people. Maybe there are potholes in the road or a fence falls over. Some of these problems are small and can be solved by one person. Others are big. They might need a group of people or someone in authority to solve them.

Directions: Draw a big problem and a small problem that could happen in your neighborhood.

Big Problem

Small Problem

Focus on Neighborhood

Responsible Decision-Making

Name: _____ Date: _____

Focus on School

Self-Awareness

Advocate for Yourself

When you are learning something new, you might not understand it at first. You might have questions. It is important to speak up for yourself in these situations. You need to advocate for yourself. Ask for help. See if the teacher will explain it again or in a different way. Do what you need to do to make sure you learn.

Directions: Create a comic strip showing what you would do if you did not understand something in school.

Name: _____ **Date:** _____

Your Teacher's Calendar

Schedules are important. They can keep people organized. Teachers use them to organize their days. Schedules help teachers finish what they need to do. A schedule also helps you as a student. It lets you know what will happen and what you will learn.

Directions: Use the teacher's schedule to answer the questions.

8:30	Class Meeting	**12:45**	Math
9:00	Reading	**1:45**	Science
10:00	Writing	**2:15**	Art
10:30	Music	**3:00**	Read Aloud
11:00	Social Studies	**3:15**	Dismissal
11:45	Lunch		

1. What is after lunch?

_____

2. How long does the class meeting last?

_____

3. Would you enjoy the morning or the afternoon more? Why?

_____

_____

4. How do you feel when you do not know your schedule? Why?

_____

_____

Name: _____ Date: _____

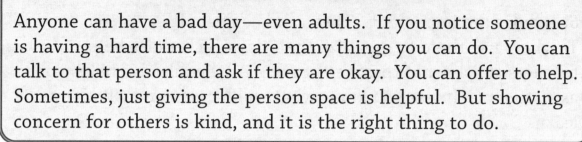

Show Concern for Others

Anyone can have a bad day—even adults. If you notice someone is having a hard time, there are many things you can do. You can talk to that person and ask if they are okay. You can offer to help. Sometimes, just giving the person space is helpful. But showing concern for others is kind, and it is the right thing to do.

Directions: Read the story. Then, draw how Isla could show kindness and concern for Miss Kent.

The Tough Morning

Isla sat quietly at her desk and looked around at her classmates. The bell had already rung, but Miss Kent was not in the classroom yet. A minute later, the teacher ran into the room. Isla noticed Miss Kent looked a little frazzled.

Miss Kent sounded out of breath. "I was running late, and then my car had a flat tire! I changed it and started to drive to school. I was going to call and tell the office I would be late, but I forgot my phone at home!"

It sounded like Miss Kent had a tough morning!

Name: _____ Date: _____

Learning around the World

Children all over the world learn in different ways. They may go to school in a building or in a home. They may learn from teachers or from family members. There are many ways to get an education. School might not be the same in different cultures, but students are still learning.

Directions: Read the text. Then, create a Venn diagram to compare your school to school in Japan.

School in Japan

Children start school in Japan when they are six years old. Elementary school lasts six years. Most students walk to school, but there are buses for those who live far away. Students arrive around 8:30 a.m. School ends around 3:30 p.m. But the students do not leave. First, they clean their classrooms. Then, most students attend a club or sport. Some of the sports they might join are baseball, soccer, judo, and kendo. Kendo is learning to use a sword. Some of the clubs are band, choir, drama, and art. They can also learn shodo, which is writing calligraphy. Students often head home around 6:00 p.m.

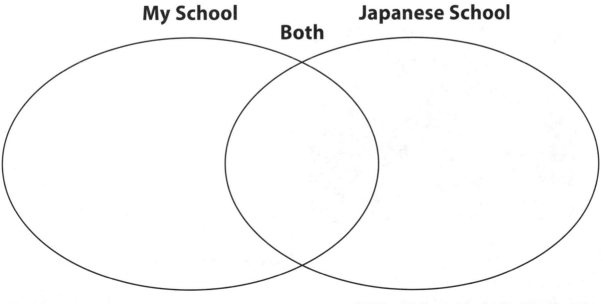

My School   **Both**   **Japanese School**

Focus on School
Relationship Skills

Name: _____ Date: _____

Anticipate Consequences

Your choices have consequences. They might be good or bad. But something will happen after every decision. You can often guess what will happen. This is called *anticipating*. Being able to anticipate can help you make wise choices.

Directions: Draw the consequence for each student's choice.

1.

2.

Name: _____ Date: _____

When Honesty Is Hard

You know it is best to be honest, but everyone makes mistakes. Sometimes, a person might tell a lie. They may have many feelings about what they did. Their body might even have a response.

Directions: Read the story. Then, answer the questions.

Accident at the Farmers Market

June wandered around the farmers market. She came to a tall pyramid of apples. She couldn't resist taking one from the edge. As she pulled the fruit, they all began to topple. June dropped the apple in her hand.

The farmer who ran the market ran over to June. "Are you okay?" he asked.

"I'm fine!" June exclaimed. "I was just walking by, and they started rolling." As she spoke, her heart pounded. Her stomach began to hurt, and her mouth felt dry.

"I'm glad you weren't hurt," the farmer said. He began picking up the apples.

1. Why do you think June did not tell the truth?

_____

_____

2. How did June's body react to her lie?

_____

_____

Name: _____ Date: _____

Self-Motivation

Some tasks are easy to finish. They might be easy, fast, or interesting. Other tasks are harder. You may not feel motivated to work on them. But they still need to be done. There are ways to motivate yourself. You might reward yourself when the task is over. You might think about how good it will feel to have the task finished. You might even give yourself a small pep talk.

Directions: Write how you would motivate yourself to complete each task.

1. Your community is spending Saturday picking up litter along the road.

   _____

   _____

2. You signed up to run a 5K to raise money for a person in your community. But you don't feel like training.

   _____

   _____

3. The food pantry in your community is running low on food. You volunteered to ask for donations door-to-door.

   _____

   _____

Name: _____ **Date:** _____

How to Be Helpful

Communities need a lot of things. They need help from the people who live there in order to thrive. Every person can do something. Your community needs you. There are many ways you can help. Helping your city or town can make it better. It can help you become a more helpful, caring person, too.

Directions: Complete the web to show how you can help your community.

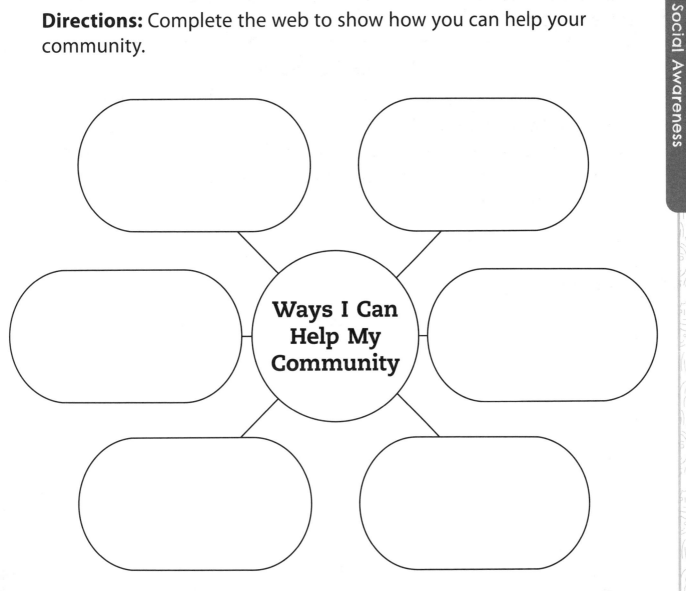

Focus on Community

Social Awareness

Name: _____ Date: _____

Focus on Community

Relationship Skills

Different People, Different Conflicts

People in communities are all different. This can create conflict. Knowing how to help solve a conflict between two people is a great skill to have. It will help you get along with others and be a help to those in need.

Directions: Read the story. Then, use the ABCD method to help solve the problem.

Dog on the Loose

Mr. Owen's dog would not stay in his yard. She kept running over to Mr. Thorne's yard to dig holes. Mr. Thorne was tired of it, and he told Mr. Owen to keep his dog in his own yard. Mr. Owen tried putting the dog on a rope when he went outside, but the dog chewed through it.

A Ask what the problem is.	
B Brainstorm ideas.	
C Choose the best one.	
D Do it. Draw your solution.	

Name: _____ Date: _____

Go to New Places

Communities have places to have fun. Even if you have lived somewhere for a long time, there are always new things to try. There might be restaurants or parks you have never visited. Maybe there is a museum or store you'd like to visit. Trying new things in your community is a great way to spend time.

Directions: Make a list of places you would like to go or things you would like to do in your community. Then, answer the question.

- _____

- _____

- _____

- _____

- _____

- _____

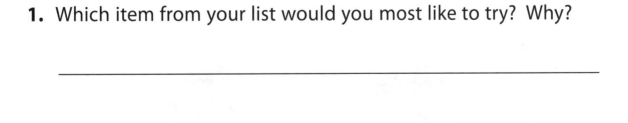

1. Which item from your list would you most like to try? Why?

_____

_____

_____

Name: _____ Date: _____

The Power of Thought

The way people think about themselves is powerful. Thinking you are brave or smart can give you confidence. Thinking you are weak or dumb can make you afraid. Try to have good feelings about yourself. It will help you do great things!

Directions: Write how you might act in each situation.

1. You are walking through your house at night. There are no lights on.

   You feel confident. _____

   _____

   You feel scared. _____

   _____

2. You have a big math test today. You studied last night.

   You feel prepared. _____

   _____

   You feel nervous. _____

   _____

Help Yourself

Helping others is great, but you also need to help yourself. You might struggle with something. It could be siblings, school, chores, or friends. It can help to think through your troubles. That is one way to be more kind to yourself.

Directions: Answer the questions about how you can help yourself.

1. What are you struggling with right now?

   _____

   _____

   _____

2. What would help you?

   _____

   _____

   _____

3. How could you help yourself?

   _____

   _____

   _____

Self-Management

Focus on Self

Name: _____ Date: _____

The Language of Gratitude

Thank you is a small phrase with a big meaning. Saying thanks is a way to show you appreciate an act or a gift from someone. There are many ways to show gratitude. You can speak it, send a message, or write a note. You can even use different languages.

Directions: Practice the different ways to say *thank you*. Then, work with a partner to thank each other in different languages.

Language	Thank You	Pronunciation
Spanish	gracias	GRAH-sy-ahs
French	merci	MEHR-see
Japanese	arigato	ah-ree-GAH-toh
Arabic	shukran	SHOW-kran
Italian	grazie	GRAHTS-yeh
Hawaiian	mahalo	ma-HA-lo
American Sign Language		

Focus on Self
Social Awareness

 126959—180 Days of Social-Emotional Learning

Name: _____ **Date:** _____

Friendship Bingo

One way to make friends is to find things you have in common. Perhaps you and another person both enjoy the same hobby or sport. That could be the start of a friendship. This is just one way to build relationships with others.

Directions: Complete the bingo board by writing your name in the center and things you enjoy in the other squares. Then, ask others you know if they enjoy any of the same things. If they do, have them sign that box on your board. See if you can get bingo.

	(your name)	

Focus on Self

Relationship Skills

Name: _____ Date: _____

A Happy, Healthy You

Your well-being has to do with how happy and healthy you are. It is good to think about your well-being. You can ask yourself questions and reflect on how you are feeling.

Directions: Answer the questions about your well-being.

1. What makes you happy?

_____

_____

2. How do you stay healthy?

_____

_____

3. How do you feel about your life right now?

_____

_____

4. Would you change anything about your life? Why or why not?

_____

_____

Name: _____ Date: _____

Your Culture Is Uniquely Yours

Your family is unique. Others may speak the same language. They might practice the same religion. But no one has a family just like yours. Learning about your family can help you learn more about yourself.

Directions: Complete as much of your family tree as you can. Add to or change the types of family members if needed.

Family Tree

_____ _____ _____ _____
(grandparent) (grandparent) (grandparent) (grandparent)

_____ _____
(parent) (parent)

_____
(me)

Name: _____ Date: _____

Manage Your Anger

Anger is a normal emotion, but it is an important feeling to manage. That helps keep situations under control. Think about two people who are angry. They might shout or use their hands. But there are better ways to handle anger. You can learn strategies to help keep things calm.

Directions: Read how to help when you feel angry. Then, answer the questions.

- Take deep breaths. Breathe in through your nose and out through your mouth.

- Be sure each person has space.

- Use a calm voice. Do not yell.

- Keep your hands and feet to yourself.

- Keep your hands loose and not balled up.

1. Describe a time you felt angry with someone in your family.

   _____

   _____

2. How could you have used the tips to manage your emotions?

   _____

   _____

   _____

   _____

Name: _____ Date: _____

The Evolution of Rules

The families you know do not all have the same rules. But what about your parents or grandparents? They were children in a different time. So they might also have had different rules. Your grandma did not have rules about a cell phone when she was little. And you might have to do different chores than your parents did. It can be fun to discover how things have changed.

Directions: Talk to an older family member about the rules they had to follow when they were young. Be sure to ask about chores they had to do, too. Then, create a Venn diagram to compare and contrast your rules with theirs.

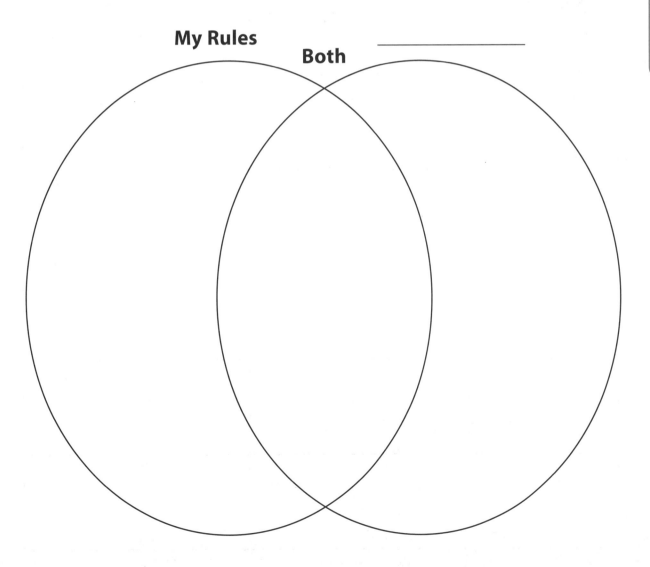

My Rules   _____
                    Both

Name: _____ Date: _____

Family Teamwork

Families often need to finish big tasks. Maybe they need to clean the basement or organize the closets. They might create a garden in the backyard or paint the walls in the house. They can work together to finish the task faster. Each person can have their own small job.

Directions: Imagine your family needs to complete a big task. List the different jobs needed to complete the task. Assign a person to each job, including yourself. Family members might need to have more than one job.

Big Task: _____

Job	Person

Focus on Family — Relationship skills

Name: _____ Date: _____

You Impact Your Family

Each member of a family has value. They may have different skills. They may have a big personality or a special talent. The blend of people is what makes a family special. Think about your family. Who is serious? Funny? Helpful? You are an important part of your family. It would not be the same without you.

Focus on Family

Responsible Decision-Making

Directions: Answer the question. Then, draw yourself and your family.

1. What good things do you bring to your family?

   _____

   _____

Name: _____ Date: _____

Intensity of Emotions

All emotions have levels. They have different intensity. Anger might feel like being annoyed. That is a low level of anger. Anger can also feel like rage. That is a high level. Knowing the levels of your feelings can help you understand yourself.

Directions: Write the emotion you would feel in each situation. Then, circle the intensity of your feeling.

> 3 = high intensity   2 = medium intensity   1 = low intensity

1. Your friend invites you over to play after school.

   emotion: _____   intensity: 3   2   1

2. Your friend breaks their arm.

   emotion: _____   intensity: 3   2   1

3. Your friend is moving to a different school.

   emotion: _____   intensity: 3   2   1

4. Your friend beats you at your favorite game.

   emotion: _____   intensity: 3   2   1

Name: _____ Date: _____

Learn to Try New Things

It can be fun to try a new activity. You can ask your friends what they like to do to get ideas.

Directions: Read the story. Then, answer the questions.

A New Interest

Myisha was looking for a new activity. She asked her friend, Trey, what she should do.

"You should try fencing," he said. Myisha looked confused, so he added, "You know, sword fighting."

"I don't know anything about that," Myisha said.

"It's so fun!" Trey exclaimed. "We travel to tournaments and wear cool uniforms. Learning to use your sword is awesome. And it's great exercise too."

Myisha looked interested. "Can I come to a practice?" she asked.

"Definitely! We have one tomorrow night."

Myisha felt excited. Maybe fencing with her friend was just what she was looking for!

1. Do you think Myisha should try fencing? Why or why not?

_____

_____

2. What kind of activity would you like to try? Why?

_____

_____

Focus on Friends

Self-Management

Name: _____ Date: _____

Learn to Show Empathy

People can have different reactions to the same event. It is important to think about how others feel. This is called *empathy*. It can make you a better friend.

Directions: Read the story. Then, answer the questions.

Making the Team

Arjun and Abir both made the basketball team.

"This is awesome!" Arjun exclaimed. "This season is going to be so much fun."

"Yeah," Abir agreed quietly. "Did you know we have practice every Monday, though?"

Arjun nodded. "And Thursdays!"

"I have band rehearsal on Mondays. I think I might have to quit, and I love playing the trumpet."

"That's a bummer," Arjun said. "But it'll be worth it to be on the team."

Abir shrugged. "I hope so."

1. How does Arjun feel about making the team?

_____

2. How does Abir feel about making the team?

_____

3. How can Arjun show empathy to Abir?

_____

Name: _____ **Date:** _____

Make a Compromise

A compromise can help end conflict. Sometimes, people want opposite things. Neither side will give in to the other. So, they compromise. Each person gives a little of what they want, and they meet in the middle. They may not get exactly what they want, but they get part of it.

Directions: Draw a compromise between two friends. Be sure to show their conflict and how they resolved it.

Name: _____ Date: _____

Focus on Friends

Responsible Decision-Making

The Gift of Gift Giving

Most people love to receive gifts, but giving gifts is fun, too. Deciding what to give a friend can be a hard choice. You need to think about what they like. Choose a budget for the gift, or make something for them. It can be helpful to think about the pros (good things) and cons (bad things) about your gift ideas. Giving a thoughtful gift is a great way to show you care.

Directions: Imagine you are giving a gift to a friend. Write two gift choices, and complete the table. Then, answer the question.

Gift Idea 1:

Pros	Cons

Gift Idea 2: _____

Pros	Cons

1. Which gift idea do you think is a better choice? Why?

_____

_____

Sense Your Emotions

You can name your emotions. You know how you feel. You can talk about what an emotion makes you think of. For example, anger might make you think of thunder. Happiness might make you think of a warm, summer day.

Directions: Write an emotion on the line. Answer the questions about it. Then, draw how you look when you are feeling that emotion.

Emotion: _____

1. Describe a time when you felt this emotion.

   _____

   _____

2. What does this emotion make you think of?

   _____

   _____

Focus on Community

Self-Awareness

Name: _____ Date: _____

Work through Emotions Together

Communities can face tough events. During these times, people often work together. They try to help and support each other. They might feel strong emotions.

Directions: Read the story. Then, answer the questions.

The Flood

Terrell had never seen anything like it. A dry summer followed by days of hard rain had flooded his city. Cars could not drive in the street. Flooded stores were closed.

Terrell and his mom volunteered to help. They stacked sandbags around buildings. They picked up trash the water left behind.

All around Terrell, people were sad. Some were upset because the flood damaged their businesses. Others were crying because their homes flooded. Everyone was tired. The cleanup was hard work. There was still so much to do.

1. How do the people in Terrell's city feel? Why?

_____

_____

2. How might the people in Terrell's city manage their emotions?

_____

_____

Name: _____ **Date:** _____

Actions Are Relative

The way a person acts is often related to how they feel. Learning how these things are related can help you see things from another person's perspective. When you can do this, you will be more patient with people.

Directions: Write how you think each person is feeling.

Person	Actions	Feelings
toddler	kicking and crying in the store	
girl	skipping at recess with a friend	
teenager	rolling eyes at parents	
adult man	tapping foot and looking at watch in line	
elderly woman	sitting in chair and changing the TV channel over and over	

Name: _____ Date: _____

Broadcast Your Communication

People can communicate in many ways. They can talk or write. They can use body language. What if they need to let an entire community know about something? One way to do this is to make flyers. Posting flyers around town means that a lot of people will see the message.

Directions: The mayor needs your help! Create a flyer for the community event based on the mayor's directions.

✉ New Email   Reply

Dear student,

Please make a flyer for the community bonfire this weekend. It will be Saturday night at 7:00 at West Lake Park. People need to bring their own blankets or chairs. The city will have ingredients for s'mores.

The flyer should have the information on it. It should also be neat and colorful.

Mayor Albridge

Focus on Community

Relationship Skills

Name: _____ **Date:** _____

Find Your Role

There are many roles in a city. There are leaders and helpers. There are volunteers who donate time. Some might be artists. Some might be organized. Each person can do something. Everyone can have a positive impact.

Directions: Draw a role you could have in your community.

Answer Key

There are many open-ended pages and writing prompts in this book. For those activities, the answers will vary. Examples are given as needed.

Week 2 Day 2 (page 18)
Examples:
1. I would tell her I ate three cookies.
2. I would tell them I broke the vase and cleaned up the mess.

Week 2 Day 5 (page 21)
1. The problem is that Josh overslept.
2. Josh could set an alarm to wake up on time.
3. Josh could ask his mom to wake him up earlier.

Week 3 Day 5 (page 26)
1. good idea; She is inviting you privately to avoid hurting anyone's feelings.
2. bad idea; Helping a stranger could be dangerous.
3. good idea: This student might be hungry and might need help to get enough food. A trusted adult can help.

Week 4 Day 2 (page 28)
1. She is afraid to tell the truth because she thinks people will be mad for not having the money for the festival and because she broke her promise.
2. It is important for her to tell the truth so people know they can trust her. It is also the right thing to do.
3. Example: I think people will understand and realize that a safe bridge is more important than a fall festival.

Week 4 Day 3 (page 29)
Examples:
1. shy: head/eyes down, blushing
2. friendly: big smile, talking to someone
3. lost: frown, crying
4. angry: scowl, yelling

Week 4 Day 5 (page 31)
Two possible problems could have been underlined:
It never has the books he wants to read.
The library does not have enough books.
Examples:
Solution 1: People in the community could donate books or money to buy new books for the library.
Solution 2: The town could ask the state for more library funding.

Week 5 Day 1 (page 32)
Examples:
1. Marcus could raise his hand and tell the teacher that he doesn't understand.
2. Bethany could explain that she doesn't have a bike and suggest doing something else.

Week 5 Day 5 (page 36)
Examples:
1. I will be tired the next day at school.
2. I will get a good grade on my quiz.
3. My sister will be upset.
4. I will make a new friend; I will make someone feel welcome.

Week 6 Day 2 (page 38)
1. Kajal feels scared.
2. I would tell Kajal to not worry that she is a child because children can come up with great ideas and make changes.
3. Kajal could make posters to hang around her neighborhood about being together in the evenings.

Week 6 Day 3 (page 39)
1. tired
2. worried/upset
3. sad/upset
4. happy

Week 6 Day 4 (page 40)
1. Examples: I could make them dinner, collect dog toys from neighbors, or bring treats for Panda.

Week 6 Day 5 (page 41)
1. Examples: Alice could practice the drums for a shorter time after breakfast or after school, and Jamal could wear ear plugs.

Week 7 Day 1 (page 42)
1. fixed mindset; Liam doesn't think he will ever be good at math.
2. growth mindset; Sofia believes hard work will help her get better at writing.

Answer Key *(cont.)*

Week 7 Day 3 (page 44)
1. school
2. both
3. both
4. home
5. school

Week 8 Day 2 (page 48)
1. Micah yelled, threatened to tattle, and waved his arm around.
2. Andre took a deep breath and counted to five. He spoke in a calm voice.

Week 8 Day 4 (page 50)

Examples:
1. They could divide the area into different sections and have each person pick up litter in their own zone.
2. They could have one person hand out plates and utensils and the other serve food.
3. They could have one person place food on the trays and the other carry the trays and pass out food.

Week 8 Day 5 (page 51)

Example: If Audrey floats on a raft, then other people may not have enough space to swim.

Week 9 Day 2 (page 53)

Examples:
1. I pictured myself calmly telling my sister what happened and apologizing. I will offer to replace the headphones.
2. I pictured myself talking to my friend and telling her about my feelings. If she doesn't want to play with me anymore, I will ask a different friend to play.

Week 9 Day 4 (page 55)
1. Yes, Jasmine is feeling peer pressure because her friends are trying to talk her into something she doesn't want to do.
2. Example: I would tell Jasmine to vote for her own choice and not give in to her friends.

Week 10 Day 1 (page 57)
1. Krish is excited. He woke up early, he can't wait to see his family, and he thinks the next five days will be awesome.

Week 10 Day 2 (page 58)
1. dinner at Grandma's; the whole family
2. Tuesday at 3:30 p.m.

Week 10 Day 5 (page 61)
1. small
2. small
3. small
4. big
5. big
6. small

Week 11 Day 1 (page 62)
1. C
2. B
3. E
4. A
5. D

Week 11 Day 2 (page 63)

Examples:
1. I feel hurt when you make fun of me.
2. I feel frustrated when you won't let me have a turn.

Week 11 Day 3 (page 64)

Examples:
1. Elliot is very excited to finally have a dog.
2. Malik is proud that his hard work paid off.
3. Alejandro is disappointed that he can't buy the game.
4. Heidi is worried that no one will pick her up.
5. Megan is hurt and thinks that they are laughing at her.

Week 11 Day 4 (page 65)
1. Tasha thinks it is unfair because Margo was allowed to ride before.
2. Tasha could talk to the teacher about Margo riding in the past. She could talk to her parents or Margo's family.

Week 11 Day 5 (page 66)

Cause: James did not play soccer after telling Lucas he would.

Effect: The two friends argued.

Answer Key (cont.)

Week 12 Day 2 (page 68)

1. I should look at the recipe again and ask someone for help. Learning new things takes time. Don't give up.
2. The park looks so much better! In just another half-hour it will be almost finished.
3. I don't really play with these toys anymore. Someone else will have fun with them, and I will really enjoy having a new recreation center.

Week 12 Day 5 (page 71)

Examples:

1. Owen could find another kind of cup to use at the coffee counter.
2. Owen could put a blanket on the ground so people could set up a display there.
3. Owen could bring them some snacks or a meal from a booth.

Week 13 Day 3 (page 74)

Examples:

1. It can be hard to accept gratitude because someone might be embarrassed or think what they did was not a big deal.
2. I should accept gratitude because it is polite and lets the other person feel heard.

Week 13 Day 4 (page 75)

1. The girl is happy.
2. The boy doesn't care or is not sure.
3. The boy is angry.
4. The girl is annoyed or frustrated.

Week 14 Day 1 (page 77)

Examples:

1. I would pick up the lid and put it back on the bin.
2. I would open the wallet, find the owner's ID, and try to return it.
3. I would ask Mr. Sanchez if I could have one tennis ball for my dog.

Week 14 Day 4 (page 80)

Examples:

1. lemons, sugar, cups, table, ice, water, pitcher, money box
2. set up table, make lemonade, pour lemonade, take money/give change

Week 15 Day 2 (page 83)

Examples:

1. No, Sura does not think she is doing anything wrong since she is only taking extra copies of the books, and the text says she is happy.
2. Yes, I think Sura is doing something wrong because she is taking something that doesn't belong to her without permission.
3. I would explain to Sura that she is stealing and that is wrong. I would tell the teacher if she continues to do it.

Week 15 Day 4 (page 85)

1. D
2. A
3. C
4. B

Week 16 Day 3 (page 89)

1. The sign needs to be fixed. The trash needs to be taken out. The frisbee needs to be taken down from the tree.

Week 17 Day 3 (page 94)

Examples:

1. Daniel's classmates and the substitute teacher probably felt irritated and distracted.
2. Leja's family probably felt sad that Leja did not want to spend time with them.
3. The club members probably felt excited to be in the club and eager to participate.

Week 18 Day 4 (page 100)

1. A Win-Lose solution is using only space or only baseball decorations.
2. A Lose-Lose solution is decorating the room in a way neither brother wants, such as with animals.
3. A Win-Win solution is each boy decorating his own space.

Week 19 Day 1 (page 102)

Examples:

1. "We have been playing basketball a lot lately. I would love to play kickball with you for a while."
2. "Are you mad at me? I feel like you are avoiding me. I want to make sure our friendship is okay."

Answer Key *(cont.)*

Week 20 Day 4 (page 110)

1. Mr. Gilt influenced Zoe with his actions. He was helping animals on his own, which made Zoe want to do it, too.
2. Mr. Gilt smiled at Zoe because he knew she was also helping animals.

Week 21 Day 2 (page 113)

Examples:

1. I may not get enough physical activity or time to play and be creative.

Week 21 Day 3 (page 114)

Examples: Do not tell anyone your real name, limit your time, only go on approved websites, tell an adult right away if you see something you shouldn't, don't share your passwords.

Week 21 Day 4 (page 115)

1. laugh out loud
2. by the way
3. for your information
4. I don't know
5. D
6. A
7. C
8. B

Week 22 Day 4 (page 120)

1. Tasha helps Miss McGee with chores. Miss McGee helps take care of Tasha.
2. Tasha learns how to cook. Miss McGee learns about the news.

Week 23 Day 2 (page 123)

1. Monday
2. Tuesday and Thursday
3. Theo should study for his test.

Week 23 Day 5 (page 126)

1. The cause was that they liked different presidents.
2. The effect was that they had a fight and stopped talking.

Week 24 Day 2 (page 128)

1. Students should circle: "I feel like it would be safer…;" "I hear what you are saying;" "I understand you are frustrated;" "I didn't think about…" Tomás used more I-messages.
2. Mark is feeling calmer and was able to see Tomás's point of view.

Week 24 Day 3 (page 129)

Examples:

1. Tessa feels proud and happy because she met a goal.
2. Carrie feels frustrated and disappointed because she trained but can't run in the race.
3. Ian feels relieved and happy because he was worried about his dog.

Week 25 Day 4 (page 135)

1. Ari is biased against the beach because he has had bad experiences with sunburns.
2. Bella is biased for the beach because she has fun building sand castles.

Week 26 Day 2 (page 138)

Examples:

1. The neighbors could set a goal to get together more often.
2. They can meet their goal by polling neighbors and then hosting something in a common area.

Week 27 Day 3 (page 144)

Examples:

1. Liz was angry because she was excited to go to Kenzie's for the first time and play the game. She didn't want to share her time with Kenzie.
2. Kenzie lives by Josie, so Josie probably comes over a lot. Kenzie may not realize how special this afternoon was to Liz.

Week 28 Day 3 (page 149)

Examples:

teacher: helpful; mayor: leader; police officer: brave; doctor: smart; banker: good at math; trash collector: strong

Answer Key *(cont.)*

Week 28 Day 4 (page 150)

1. Mr. Miller needs help because gardening makes him sore and tired.

2. Example: Mr. Miller could talk to people who enjoy gardening. He could put up a poster. He could talk to a community leader about finding someone new.

Week 29 Day 3 (page 154)

1. Cade is upset because he didn't study for his spelling test.

2. Example: Cade could tell himself that everyone forgets things when they are busy. He could tell himself to try his best and sound out the words and that he'll do better next time.

Week 29 Day 5 (page 156)

Examples:

1. The dog leash was missing; She could call the family, and ask where it is.

2. The dog spilled water; She could get a towel and clean it up.

3. The dog food is almost gone; She could ask a parent to take her to the store to buy more.

Week 30 Day 2 (page 158)

1. Katya's fear was that the new girl wouldn't like her.

2. Katya went outside to say hello to the girl even though she was nervous.

Week 30 Day 3 (page 159)

Examples:

1. A teacher might feel excited because they want to meet their students.

2. A third-grader might feel disappointed because they love the freedom of summer.

3. A parent might feel happy to get their children back in school.

4. A kindergartner might feel nervous because it is their first time going to school.

Week 30 Day 4 (page 160)

Examples:

1. I could wave.

2. I could shrug my shoulders.

3. I could pant or wipe my hand across my forehead.

4. I could wrap my arms around myself and shiver.

5. I could tap my wrist with my finger.

Week 31 Day 2 (page 163)

1. math

2. 30 minutes

Week 32 Day 1 (page 167)

1. Example: June was worried she would get in trouble. She may have been embarrassed.

2. June's heart beat fast, her stomach hurt, and her mouth was dry.

Week 32 Day 4 (page 170)

A. The problem is Mr. Owen's dog is digging holes in the neighbor's yard.

B. Examples: Mr. Owen could put up a fence, install an invisible fence, or use a chain instead of a rope.

Week 35 Day 3 (page 184)

1. Arjun is excited about making the basketball team.

2. Abir is unsure about making the basketball team.

3. Example: Arjun could tell Abir that he knows it's a tough decision for him.

Week 36 Day 2 (page 188)

Examples:

1. The people are sad and angry because the flooding has damaged their town.

2. They could try to think about positive things, such as there are many people helping and everyone is safe.

Week 36 Day 3 (page 189)

toddler: angry/upset

girl: happy

teenager: frustrated/annoyed

man: impatient

woman: bored

References Cited

The Aspen Institute: National Commission on Social, Emotional, & Academic Development. 2018. "From a Nation at Risk to a Nation at Hope." https://nationathope.org/wp-content/uploads/2018_aspen_final-report_full_webversion.pdf.

Collaborative for Academic, Social, and Emotional Learning (CASEL). n.d. "What Is SEL?" Last modified December 2020. https://casel.org/what-is-sel/.

Durlak, Joseph A., Roger P. Weissberg, Allison B. Dymnicki, Rebecca D. Taylor, and Kriston B. Schellinger. 2011. "The Impact of Enhancing Students' Social and Emotional Learning: A Meta-Analysis of School-Based Universal Interventions." *Child Development* 82 (1): 405–32.

Goleman, Daniel. 2005. *Emotional Intelligence: Why It Can Matter More Than IQ.* New York: Bantam Dell.

Palmer, Parker J. 2007. *The Courage to Teach: Exploring the Inner Landscape of a Teacher's Life.* San Francisco: Jossey-Bass.

Name: _____ Date: _____

Connecting to Self Rubric

Days 1 and 2

Directions: Complete this rubric every six weeks to evaluate students' Day 1 and Day 2 activity sheets. Only one rubric is needed per student. Their work over the six weeks can be considered together. Appraise their work in each category by circling or highlighting the descriptor in each row that best describes the student's work. Then, consider the student's overall progress in connecting to self. In the box, draw ☆, ✓+, or ✓ to indicate your overall evaluation.

Competency	Advanced	Satisfactory	Developing
Self-Awareness	Can accurately identify one's own full range of emotions.	Identifies one's own emotions accurately most of the time.	Has trouble identifying their own feelings.
	Understands that thoughts and feelings are connected.	Sees the connection of thoughts and feelings most of the time.	Does not connect thoughts to feelings.
	Can identify strengths and areas of growth.	Can identify a few strengths and weaknesses.	Can identify only one strength or weakness.
Self-Management	Can manage stress by using several different strategies.	Manages stress with only one strategy.	Does not manage stress well.
	Shows motivation in all areas of learning.	Shows motivation in a few areas of learning.	Shows little to no motivation.
	Is able to set realistic goals.	Sets some goals that are realistic and some that are not.	Has a hard time setting goals that are achievable.

Comments   **Overall**

_____

_____

_____

_____

Name: _____ Date: _____

Relating to Others Rubric

Days 3 and 4

Directions: Complete this rubric every six weeks to evaluate students' Day 3 and Day 4 activity sheets. Only one rubric is needed per student. Their work over the six weeks can be considered together. Appraise their work in each category by circling or highlighting the descriptor in each row that best describes the student's work. Then, consider the student's overall progress in relating to others. In the box, draw ☆, ✓+ , or ✓ to indicate your overall evaluation.

Competency	Advanced	Satisfactory	Developing
Social Awareness	Shows empathy toward others.	Shows empathy toward others most of the time.	Shows little to no empathy toward others.
	Can explain how rules are different in different places.	Knows that some places can have different rules.	Is not able to articulate how rules may change in different places.
	Can list many people who support them in their learning.	Can list some people who support them in their learning.	Can list few people who support them in their learning.
Relationship Skills	Uses a variety of strategies to solve conflicts with peers.	Has a few strategies to solve conflicts with peers.	Struggles to solve conflicts with peers.
	Uses advanced skills of listening and paraphrasing while communicating.	Is able to communicate effectively.	Has breakdowns in communication skills.
	Works effectively with a team. Shows leadership in accomplishing team goals.	Works effectively with a team most of the time.	Has trouble working with others on a team.

Comments

Overall

_____

_____

_____

_____

Name: _____ Date: _____

Making Decisions Rubric

Day 5

Directions: Complete this rubric every six weeks to evaluate students' Day 5 activity sheets. Only one rubric is needed per student. Their work over the six weeks can be considered together. Appraise their work in each category by circling or highlighting the descriptor in each row that best describes the student's work. Then, consider the student's overall progress in making decisions. In the box, draw ☆, ✓+ , or ✓ to indicate your overall evaluation.

Competency	Advanced	Satisfactory	Developing
Responsible Decision-Making	Makes decisions that benefit their own long-term interests.	Makes decisions that are sometimes impulsive and sometimes thought out.	Is impulsive and has a hard time making constructive choices.
	Knows how to keep self and others safe in a variety of situations.	Knows how to keep themselves safe in most situations.	Is capable of being safe, but sometimes is not.
	Is able to consider the consequences of their actions, both good and bad.	Is able to identify some consequences of their actions.	Struggles to anticipate possible consequences to their actions.

Comments

_____

_____

_____

Overall

☐

Connecting to Self Analysis

Directions: Record each student's overall symbols (page 198) in the appropriate columns. At a glance, you can view: (1) which students need more help mastering these skills and (2) how students progress throughout the school year.

Student Name	Week 6	Week 12	Week 18	Week 24	Week 30	Week 36

Relating to Others Analysis

Directions: Record each student's overall symbols (page 199) in the appropriate columns. At a glance, you can view: (1) which students need more help mastering these skills and (2) how students progress throughout the school year.

Student Name	Week 6	Week 12	Week 18	Week 24	Week 30	Week 36

Making Decisions Analysis

Directions: Record each student's overall symbols (page 200) in the appropriate columns. At a glance, you can view: (1) which students need more help mastering these skills and (2) how students progress throughout the school year.

Student Name	Week 6	Week 12	Week 18	Week 24	Week 30	Week 36

Digital Resources

Accessing the Digital Resources

The Digital Resources can be downloaded by following these steps:

1. Go to **www.tcmpub.com/digital**

2. Use the ISBN number to redeem the Digital Resources.

3. Respond to the question using the book.

4. Follow the prompts on the Content Cloud website to sign in or create a new account.

5. Choose the Digital Resources you would like to download. You can download all the files at once, or a specific group of files.

ISBN:
9781087649726

Notes

Notes

Notes

Notes